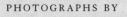

PHOTOGRAPHS BY

KRIS TIMKEN

Gay Dads

Gay Dads

A CELEBRATION OF FATHERHOOD

David Strah

with Susanna Margolis

Jeremy P. Tarcher/Putnam
a member of Penguin Group (USA) Inc.
New York

Most Tarcher/Putnam books are available at special quantity discounts for bulk purchase for sales promotions, premiums, fund-raising, and educational needs. Special books or book excerpts also can be created to fit specific needs. For details, write Penguin Group (USA) Inc. Special Markets, 375 Hudson Street, New York, NY 10014.

Jeremy P. Tarcher/Putnam
a member of
Penguin Group (USA) Inc.
375 Hudson Street
New York, NY 10014
www.penguin.com

Library of Congress Cataloging-in-Publication Data

Strah, David.
Gay Dads : a celebration of fatherhood / by David Strah ; with Susanna Margolis.
p.   cm.
ISBN 1-58542-231-2
1. Gay fathers—United States—Case studies.   2. Gay fathers—United States—Family
relationships.   I. Margolis, Susanna.   II. Title.
HQ76.13.S77   2003   2002043048
306.874'2—dc21

Printed in the United States of America
1   3   5   7   9   10   8   6   4   2

Book design by Amanda Dewey

For Barry,

who makes my dreams come true,

And for Zev and Summer,

who are my dream.

ACKNOWLEDGMENTS

I t's a pleasure to express my thanks to a number of people who provided inspiration, information, and numerous intangible forms of assistance in the creation of this book.

Special thanks to Michael Sheldon for laying the groundwork on which the book was built.

Thanks also to Maggie Drucker for her friendship and professional assistance.

To Kris Timken, whose photographs bring the people in this book to life, I offer particular thanks. Without her dedication, commitment, and enthusiasm, and without endless travel that took her from her family, this book simply would not have happened. She consistently exceeded expectations. To my agent, Sarah Jane Freymann, who believed in the project from the beginning and kept on believing in it through thick and thin, and to Susanna Margolis, who helped give voice to so many gay dads, I express deepest gratitude.

Joel Fotinos, publisher of the Jeremy P. Tarcher imprint, and editor Sara Carder have been unwavering in their enthusiasm for the book and were always available to provide sound guidance and assistance. I am very grateful to them both.

To Kelly Groves, of Penguin's public relations department, and to PR gurus Jim Long, Merrill Rose, and David Zucker, warmest thanks for all your efforts. Thanks also to Howard Lesman for putting me in touch with Merrill and David—and for your support.

I extend particular gratitude to Sally Susman, communications maven extraordinaire, for her commitment and enthusiasm in spearheading the effort to get the word out about *Gay Dads*.

I want also to acknowledge the support and love—given both to my family and to this project—by my parents, Joyce McKelvey and Michael and Sara Penn-Strah, by my in-laws, Ruth and Ron Miguel, and by my sister Annie and sisters-in-law Melanie and Renée. I am grateful to you all.

For their friendship, as consistent as it is profound, I thank MaryAnn Deffenbaugh and Catherine Ryan.

Thanks also to Terry Boggis, director of Center Kids, and to staff at COLAGE and the Human Rights Campaign for referring families to be interviewed.

To Maris Blechner, the executive director of Family Focus, the adoption agency for my own family, and to attorney Michael Goldstein and legal assistant Renée Franklin, endless thanks for helping to create my family and for their invaluable help in clarifying numerous points of information.

Dr. Stephanie Schacher, Psy.D., generously articulated the findings of her research and shared her own perspective in the matter of the "new gay dads." Her pioneering research, articulated in her doctoral thesis, *Fathering Experiences of the "New" Gay Fathers: A Qualitative Research Study,* illumines a growing and important phenomenon.

Thanks also to researchers Lauren Hudecki, of the Lambda Legal Defense and Education Fund, and Nikki Cruz, of COLAGE, for prompt, thorough research—congenially delivered.

I want to express my eternal gratitude to the birthmothers of my children—and to all the birthmothers of all the children. Your sacrifice is our greatest gift, and you will always have a place in all our hearts.

Finally, thanks to all the fathers who agreed to be interviewed for the book—for their time and for generously sharing their experiences.

Contents

Gay Dads

Gay Dads:
A New Phenomenon
in the American Family

I n our statistics-happy nation, there are as yet no precise figures beyond crude estimates that measure the number of gay men who have set out to have children and create families of their own. Perhaps nobody has yet been able to count these men, for they represent a new phenomenon in our society.

To be sure, there have always been men who married, fathered children with their wives, and only later—or perhaps never—identified themselves as homosexual. In the past, many such men probably remained closeted all their lives. More recently, many have come out of the closet and out of their marriages, while of course remaining devoted fathers to their children. But the phenomenon of men who identify themselves as gay, who openly and publicly live gay lives, and who *then* undertake to create families is still a fledgling trend.

When my partner and I, an openly gay couple, became fathers for the first time in 1998, I felt that my heart was going to burst with joy and new-found love for our son. But I also felt isolated as a gay dad. I couldn't find anyone else like me in what was otherwise a vibrantly cosmopolitan city. I knew instinctively that there must be other families like mine, and I wanted to see them, hear from them, learn about their troubles and triumphs, find out what we had in common and what was different about their experience. I suspect that other gay dads feel a similar isolation, wherever they may live. It's why I wrote this book.

In it, you'll meet 44 of the "new" gay dads, fathers in 24 families. You'll hear what they went through to form their families, how they feel about what they went through, how they view parenting as gay men in the twenty-first century. I hope the book gives readers a sense of being present at the beginning of what I expect will one day become a more common aspect of gay life.

To find these families, I alerted a number of national and local gay organizations. I received more than a hundred responses, interviewed more than 60 gay dads, and winnowed the number down to the 23 families in this book—24, including my own. I also sought out the assistance of a seasoned professional writer, Susanna Margolis, who helped with the interviewing, gave shape to the individual stories, and brought to the task the perspective of someone from outside the gay community.

Who are the men in this book? They are as diverse a bunch as you'll find anywhere in our diverse nation. When Rosie O'Donnell famously "came out" on national television, she told Diane Sawyer, "I don't think America knows what a gay parent looks like: I am the gay parent." So are the men in this book. They are of different races and skin colors. Professionals, wage-earners, and full-time homemakers. Young and middle-aged. Deeply religious and mildly observant. Tall and short, athletes and couch potatoes, activists and homebodies. They come from all parts of the country. The 2000 U.S. census conclusively dispelled the notion that gay men live only in the well-known urban centers of both coasts—New York, San Francisco, Los Angeles. These profiles bring the census figures to life, especially, in my view, in showing the trend to suburban life. Evidently, gay dads seek the same two-car garages, tree-lined streets, and collegial neighborhoods that have long been a model of American family life. It brings home the real answer to the question of who these men are: whether you're gay or straight, they're your neighbors.

But the experience they bring to the neighborhood is a distinctive one. For while the diversity among these gay dads is striking, even more striking are the commonalities. Read through these profiles, and certain themes recur—page after page. I think of these common themes as the "findings" of my exploration into the lives of gay fathers and their families.

Perhaps the most moving theme—a persistent if not universal finding—is the sense of miracle so many of these men feel at being fathers. Profile after profile speaks of how the joy of coming out as a gay man was tempered by regret that it meant a public farewell to parenthood—or so it was assumed. If the life stories in this book tell you nothing else, surely they proclaim that it is possible for gay men to be fathers. It is possible, it is practicable, and it is our fundamental right as human beings.

But becoming a father can sometimes be a Herculean task. You will read in this book about adoption—public, private, domestic, and international; about surrogacy; about coparenting. You will meet men who became fathers as a couple and others who are single dads. You will read about the different processes each of these avenues to fatherhood entails—the waiting, the preparation, the often intrusive evaluation of the men and their homes, the bureaucracies that must be dealt with, the false leads, the very painful discrimination, the high price of seeing a pregnancy through, or of flying overseas to bring home an internationally adopted child, or of the surrogacy process. Yet in every case, the men in this book stuck it out, kept struggling, claimed their rights, and triumphed in the end. In my mind, they are heroic, and their heroism is a gift for their children.

Many of those children are multiracial, creating lots of families that transcend race. It is a situation not without controversy. But I think it is fair to say of these families that their gay fathers, having faced discrimination and isolation for their sexuality, possess resources for handling the situation that others might lack.

In that regard, another of the themes that threads through these profiles is the healing impact of fatherhood. Especially for those men estranged from their families and thus in a way cut off from their own childhoods, becoming a parent appears to be restorative, even therapeutic. If it does not remedy the estrangement, it is such an optimistic plunge into the future that it can overwhelm the pain of the past.

Ironically, however, fatherhood can "cause" another kind of isolation—this time from the gay community. Of course, it's understandable that these gay dads suddenly feel more in tune with the straight parents of their children's friends than with their old friends; after all, they have joined the Tribe of Parents. What is less easy to compute is the fathers' sense that their gay friends are no longer interested in them, a recognition that becoming parents has so changed their lives and sensibilities that they no longer "fit" in that community—or at least, that the community doesn't seem to think they fit. This is a phenomenon that is both puzzling and sad, but it is widely felt by the men in this book.

My partner and I have felt it, as I'll relate in our story, and I have thought a lot about it. To me, the equivocal reaction to gay dads by many in the gay community—an indifference that sometimes approaches resentment—is just one more indication that parenthood signals a sea change in our community.

The details of the change are only now beginning to be studied—thus far by only a small handful of pioneering researchers. Dr. Stephanie Schacher, a licensed clinical psychologist practicing here in New York, is one of the pioneers.* Her findings affirm that the new fatherhood is having an impact not just on the lives of the gay dads themselves but also on the life of the gay community.

For one thing, fatherhood is stretching the lives and perspectives of the new gay dads beyond the gay community, Schacher says, "connecting them to the community at large." It provides a bridge to the heterosexual world, is often the basis of "better relations with extended families," and offers the men "a comfort and commonality they did not have before." It is also, she says, "an important personal growth experience." Her study found that gay dads felt fatherhood had unleashed capacities for giving and loving they had not known they possessed. It also made them "feel better about their own identity," Schacher says, "helping eradicate any remnant of their own internalized homophobia." There are similar revelations from some of the men in this book, men who say they feel

---

*Others include Dr. Schacher's colleague Dr. Barbara Quartironi and, in the United Kingdom, Gillian A. Dunne. I am grateful to Dr. Schacher for permission both to cite her 2000 doctoral dissertation, *Fathering Experiences of the "New" Gay Fathers: A Qualitative Research Study,* and to quote our conversation.

more at ease with their own sexuality, more linked to the world at large through fatherhood.

At the same time, Schacher found that gay dads see themselves as "writing their own script" for parenthood, freed from ties to traditional gender roles. "They are generalists rather than specialists" in parenting, she says. "They blend the daddy and mommy roles into one totality, then split the totality into parental roles and allocate those roles by inclination or talent or convenience." In so doing, she adds, gay dads are "redefining masculine gender roles, too, just by doing it. They are modeling a new masculine gender role of nurturing, empathy, caretaking, and expressing emotion." And, I would add, we are doing this in a very public way—at school, in the playground, in community interaction. It's why I am occasionally asked if I am my children's nanny, or where my wife is, or if I'm the uncle. Some people simply can't easily conceptualize a full-time gay dad.

What I found particularly intriguing was Schacher's response to the results of her research. Having begun her study "neither pro nor con the idea of gay dads," in her words, she emerged from the work with the sense that "this is how everybody should embark on being a parent." For most straight people, Schacher goes on, becoming a parent "is like going to school. Everybody does it, but without really thinking about it." Yet "parenting is one of the most important functions in life," something for which people "should be emotionally, mentally, psychologically prepared," something that "takes a lot of work, doesn't happen overnight, and deserves some prior soul-searching."

That, she says, is precisely what new gay dads bring to parenting: forethought, homework, exploration of their motives, consideration of how to carry out the parenting task, deliberate and careful and loving preparation. It makes the new gay fathers "a model," Schacher says, "of what parenting should be about."

The model creates a whole new role for gay men as well—and a whole new departure for the gay community. For *as* a community, we have not seen parenting as part of our milieu. Fatherhood has been a circumstance well outside the conditions of our lives, well beyond the tribal walls we erected for safety, security, and the freedom to live our lives honestly.

One of the men profiled in this book says that gay men having children is a sign that they are growing up. I agree with him. If coming out was the first step and forming a movement the second, then perhaps asserting our fundamental right to be parents is the third step in our evolution as a community. It's a step out of the ghetto-like colonies many of us understandably walked into when we came out as gay men. Like any next step, that can be dangerous. It can be frightening. But as the men in this book make clear, fatherhood is worth it.

Naysayers, False Starts,
and Works of Art

Sometimes "the whole process is fraught with naysayers," says Larry Leon. He and his partner, Marc Salans, should know. Throughout their process of adopting children, they were confronted by negative attitudes, doubts, and would-be dissuaders.

Starting with themselves.

Salans and Leon had been together some six years when they began to talk about becoming parents. At first they couldn't even get together on whether this was something they wanted or not. When one of them was up on the idea, the other was down. Then vice versa. Finally the pendulum steadied, and they were together in their determination to go forward.

There followed a year of research into what Salans calls "the options for potential gay dads." A lawyer for the government, Salans is adept at such research. He "read everything he could get his hands on and talked to every person and every agency he could find," his partner says. The result was "a stack six feet tall sitting in the kitchen," but the work paid off. As the stack expanded, the men's focus on what they wanted and how to go about it grew sharper.

They nixed the idea of surrogacy. For one thing, says Marc, "we lived in D.C. at the time, where surrogacy did not seem legal"; at least, Marc found, the issue was murky at best. Cost was another concern; their calculations reckoned surrogacy at twice the price of adoption. They also were uneasy about public adoption through a welfare agency. For one thing, "having an infant in the house was important to us," says Larry Leon, and they would not necessarily be able to "order" a newborn if they went through the public system. They also had concerns about what Leon calls the "risk" of public adoption. In the management lingo that comes naturally to him—Leon helps run a large commercial landscaping company—he explains their view "that raising a kid was already a risk-laden adjustment with no guarantees. With public adoption, the risk would be even greater."

They were leaning to the choice of open adoption, but when a gay parenting conference was held in nearby Baltimore, they went along to learn what they could. They "learned" that their "only option," according to the social worker at the lectern, was "to adopt a special-needs child." Marc raised his hand. "What about open adoption?" he asked. "Good luck," retorted the social worker. "No one will turn over a baby to a gay couple."

"That was 1996," Marc remarks. "A lot has changed since then."

Meanwhile, the men had signed on with an agency they were referred to by New York's Center Kids, which advocates at state and local levels for the rights of alternative families. The agency, the Vermont-based Friends in Adoption, specializes in domestic open adoption and sponsored a weekend on the subject for prospective parents—gay and straight. As it turned out, Marc and Larry were the only gay couple there, but after all the naysaying they had been through, the positive things they heard at the weekend made it a "great experience." What they heard was how psychologically healthy open adoption can be for both the birthmother and the child: the birthmother can both choose her child's parents and decide whether and how much to develop or maintain a relationship with them, while the adoptive parents can find out what they need to know about their child's birthparents.

Leon and Salans were sold. They "put together a brochure for the prospective birthmother," Leon relates. "It had pictures of our life, an explanation of who we were and what we're about, and our hopes and dreams for our child." They also put the adoption brochure on-line, under the search term "seeking to adopt." They got an 800 number at their house so they could answer the responses themselves, but after nightly harassing calls, they had all responses forwarded to the agency in Vermont. And they advertised in *Rolling Stone,* among whose hip and forward-thinking readership they hoped to find a sympathetic ear.

They did. But first there were two false starts. In both cases, they had prolonged involvements with the women, both of whom seemed intelligent, rational, and amiable. Yet one was "a total kook playing us like a fiddle," says Salans, and the other turned out to be "a crazy woman who worked in a hospital and falsified medical records confirming her pregnancy." There was no such pregnancy, and even though the men had

been warned by their agency that these kinds of things could happen, the experiences brought them to their "emotional bottom."

"By now we were two years into the process," Larry says. "We were frustrated and beginning to think it was all fruitless. And we were at our wits' end about what to do next. We were thinking about changing gears, maybe going the international adoption route, or surrogacy. We were just second-guessing ourselves all over the place." They decided to go up to Vermont, meet with the adoption agency staff, and reassess everything.

"You're never going to believe this," the head of the agency said to them when they arrived in the southwestern corner of Vermont on a sparkling spring day. There had been a response to the *Rolling Stone* ad from a 17-year-old girl in Georgia. She was white, her boyfriend was black, and neither was prepared or equipped to take on the responsibilities of parenthood. What's more, the expectant mother had been particularly attracted by the fact that a pair of "hopeful" gay dads, as the ad put it, "want to share their life with your newborn."

Marc and Larry had been adamant that the ad make clear they were gay. That was "very important to us both," Larry explains. One of the reasons they had ruled out international adoption, for example, "was that we would have had to lie about being gay, about who and what we are. And we refused to do that. We wanted to go through the process openly and honestly."

To the 17-year-old pregnant girl in Georgia, their being gay was a plus. She lived with her lesbian mother and the mother's partner and was comfortable with that. She also knew that gay couples had a harder time adopting than straight couples, so to her, "this was the right thing to do." And perhaps also, like the staff at the adoption agency, she felt that a biracial child would do best with adoptive parents who were likely to have had personal knowledge of intolerance.

There was one catch. It's what the agency head had meant when she said: "You're never going to believe this." The expected biracial child was actually twins—a boy and a girl.

Marc and Larry didn't think about it too long. They had talked about having two kids—eventually. Now "eventually" would come right away; that was all.

But the men remained wary about the pregnancy. They had been badly burned before, so when "a couple of things didn't add up" in their phone conversations with the Georgia teenager, the agency suggested they fly there to meet with her face-to-face.

In the poem-story Marc wrote to tell his children about their adoption, he speaks of the meeting at a Red Lobster restaurant, how they talked with the young woman

> *for two hours about things serious and funny.*
> *They talked about (her) interests, like photography and crocheting,*
> *About her plans for the future, about the options she was weighing.*
> *(She) said: "I'm not ready to raise a child, let alone two.*
> *I'm only seventeen, and wouldn't know what to do.*
> *Through adoption I can give them the life they deserve,*
> *Full of laughter and joy, and love without reserve."*

Marc and Larry liked the young woman. They found her smart, pretty, and engaging—and they confirmed that she was pregnant. Six months pregnant. The men went home to Washington to wait.

The call came from their birthmother's mother's partner. By the time Leon and Salans arrived at the hospital in Atlanta, the babies had been born. "They were," says Larry, "the two most beautiful babies you'd ever want to see." Marc agrees.

They spent two days at the hospital with the birthmother and a number of her family members. It was "very intimate," Salans says, "unique, different from anything we expected." Yet the two men remained on tenterhooks. They knew that the birthmother could still change her mind. Their lawyer in Georgia had told them that many obstetric nurses tended to be "antiadoption" and tried to dissuade birthmothers from signing relinquishment papers. In fact, that's exactly what was going on in their case. And the twins' birthmother had plenty of time to listen. Because the delivery had been by C-section, she was still under the influence of painkillers, which meant that she couldn't sign any papers lest they be legally challenged. Against the nurses' importunings, the men felt impotent. All they had to counter the antiadoption argument was their yearning to be parents and the intense love they already felt for these babies.

It was like waiting for the jury to decide your fate. Tired of sitting by the phone in their hotel room, Salans and Leon headed for the mall, cell phone in hand. When it rang, they held their breath. It was their lawyer, telling them that the papers had been signed. In the middle of the mall, the two men hugged and wept. They were the legal guardians of Jonathan and Emily.

They also got a call from the birthmother as she was leaving the hospital. She wanted to say goodbye and thanks but broke down as she did so. Larry broke down too, "realizing the enormity of what she had done." In the story-poem, the men thank her in these words:

"You've given us the most precious gifts we've ever received before.
Whenever we lay eyes on them, our hearts begin to soar.
We've only known them a few short days, but already we love them so.
Thank you for making our dreams come true, like some angel with a
halo."

Their dreams had come true, but so had the reality of being stuck in a hotel room with two newborns for 10 days while the adoption was processed. My God, Marc thought, what have we done? Overnight, life flipped 180 degrees. But in fact, the 10 days were "neat." A sister of a coworker came to visit and brought dinners. They remembered that people they had met on a vacation lived in Atlanta. And rank strangers "were very supportive and loving," including all the women who worked at the hotel who wanted to "see the twins."

The one fly in the ointment was the grandparents—both sets. Although Marc's parents are "enlightened and pretty liberal about most things, there is an ingrained homophobia there, an old-fashioned belief about what it means to be gay—namely, that all gay people are unhappy." That "homophobia" surfaced early on in the adoption process when Marc wrote them about his plans to adopt and asked if they would be willing to help financially. They were not, and the reason, as Marc eventually elicited it, was their fear that a child of gay parents could not grow up happy, would not be accepted by his peers, and would be forever scarred psychologically. After an exchange of letters, the relationship was sorely strained, and Marc's father began to ask what he could do to mend it.

Larry's father, who originally claimed he found the adoption "no big deal," made a number of objections once the reality loomed. These kids will have enough problems being biracial, he warned his son; their troubles will multiply if they have gay parents.

Both men communicated back to their parents that, in Larry's words, "This is what we're doing, and you're going to have to accept it." When the men returned home from Atlanta with Jonathan and Emily, Larry's parents were there, and "the minute they set eyes on the kids, they were their grandparents." Marc's parents, who live in France, also came around. They loved the children sight unseen; when they finally did see them, as they do annually when the Leon-Salans family visits Paris, they waxed ecstatic about children who "could not look better or happier" and about the fine job of parenting by their fathers.

The kids are totally different from one another, says Larry. Emily is "very feminine and flirtatious. She loves to dress up and play the coquette. Jonathan is a rough-and-tumble bundle of testosterone. On the other hand, Emily is fearless and absolutely stoic, while Jonathan is frightened of the dark and cries more readily."

The family lives a life that Marc describes as "pretty boring, pretty regular." They have a station wagon and a golden retriever and are friends with all the other parents in the neighborhood. They're the only gay dads in the neighborhood, and Marc says "it's been a nonissue." They take the kids to the playground and the swimming pool, read to them a lot, hope to expose them to a range of life's possibilities. "They've been to France three times by the age of four," Marc says. "That's what we want to do for our kids. It has nothing to do with our being gay dads."

Naturally, it isn't all unalloyed joy. Larry remembers the "abject despair" he felt when the twins were misdiagnosed with a disease found in HIV-positive babies. "We went through 10 days of finding out what was wrong. It was horrible, stressful. Waiting for the results of their AIDS tests was agony." It all turned out all right, but Larry says that the range of emotions he experienced was "eye-opening."

"I grew up with a lot of angst about being gay," Larry explains. "It was difficult coming to terms with it over the years, and I may not be totally at terms with it now. But having kids has been a healing experience. It has allowed me to recognize that I really am no different from everybody else. All the things you know intellectually I now experience"—all those clichés about parental love. "I am more at ease with myself, more at ease in the world." For Marc, being a parent is harder than he expected—"not because I'm a gay man, just because it's hard"—but it "surpasses anything" he ever imagined.

Sometimes, people ask if the kids have a Latino mother. "No," one or the other will answer. "She's white." "Then who's that other guy?" people will want to know. "What's going on?" "That's my partner," they will answer. "It's important," says Larry, "for the kids never to sense discomfort about us being gay." He wishes they had "more interaction with gay families," and they've made a point of trying to find other gay and lesbian couples with children and of exposing the kids to African-Americans and biracial individuals. It's a "conscious decision to show them other families like theirs and other people like themselves."

And then there's the time Marc was in the supermarket with the kids, and a woman walked up to him and said: "Your children are works of art."

Even Better
Than They Planned

When is the perfect moment to have a child? Fred Gabriel and Michael Deveau were pretty sure they knew. So sure, in fact, that they planned their lives around it.

At their first meeting in 1994, they talked about a shared dream of becoming fathers. Michael was living in Boston at the time, and Fred was in the New York area, but when Michael showed up in New York and the two had their first real "date," it was at a meeting of gay parents. Says Fred: "It was strange to be sitting there with a guy I hardly knew. We learned a lot about each other."

Five months later, they moved in together and began to lay out what Michael calls "a plan to prepare ourselves for becoming parents. First, we were going to move back to New England and buy a house. Then we would open a business together. Then we would start the adoption process."

In 1994, the pair duly moved to a town some 40 miles north of Boston, buying a house that "needed work." In 1999 they opened a candle and gift store, CityWicks; running a store, they reasoned, would free one of them to take a child to the doctor or drive him or her to an activity. Fred also worked as a financial reporter for *Investment News,* a job that could often be done from home. One by one, they were ticking off the agenda items on their to-do list for parenthood.

But "we kept adding things that should be done," says Michael. "We kept waiting for the perfect moment to begin the adoption process." Fred began to feel that they were "front-loading the situation to be perfect" and thus "pushing back the moment" of starting the process.

Doubts began to set in. Michael was nearing 40, a substantial milestone in its own right, and he began to wonder aloud if "maybe I'd be fine not having children." Fred, four years younger, urged him to take the opposite approach: "You're pushing 40, and if we're going to do this, let's do it." At best, they were at different points on the same wavelength; at worst, the wavelength was diverging into different frequencies.

Then one day when Fred was surfing the Internet, he dropped in on a gay parents listserv and saw the following posting:

"Hi, folks! There is a baby boy in Cambodia named Veayo, born November 1999, who needs a home. He was born with a cleft lip and palate, just like my first son, also from Cambodia, and I'm eager to find him a family. Cleft palate repair surgery is routine in developed countries but unavailable in Cambodia. If anyone is interested, write me for more info. Thanks, Julie."

Fred shot back a message to the effect that he and his partner were "very interested," and he asked for "more info on the young boy in Cambodia." In no time at all, Julie had put him in touch with the Seattle-based adoption agency with connections to the Cambodian orphanage. It was January 28, 2000, the start of a process that would take seven months to complete.

Yet even with the process well and truly underway, uncertainty continued to hover over the Gabriel-Deveau household. While Fred was communicating daily with Julie, the agency, and three other would-be adoptive parents of cleft-lip-and-palate children from Cambodia, the Fred-Michael wavelength was oscillating all over the place. The two had begun seeing a couples counselor—not over any particular grievance but rather "as part of a six-year maintenance check," in Fred's phrase. Now the adoption became the central topic of their counseling sessions. "I talked about Michael lagging," says Fred, "about his not being with me on the adoption. I had found this Cambodian child, and now he was putting up obstacles. I was frustrated, feeling like fatherhood was becoming unobtainable."

For his part, Michael "was looking at our old house that leaked like a sieve, and I said we have to do these things to get ready. We need to put up new windows. We need to do all the things that a good homestudy would require. I wasn't suggesting we stop the process; I just wanted us to be prepared."

The fact that they were seeking to adopt a specific child made their adoption case different, but it did not seem to lessen the paperwork burden or speed the process. It took six months to submit all the paperwork to the Immigration and Naturalization Service (INS) for clearance; the agency then proceeded to lose their paperwork, which they had to resubmit. They hired a private homestudy agency to evaluate their home and do all the necessary background checks; that took three months.

In the midst of all this, a picture of their prospective child arrived in the mail. In fact, it arrived on the very day they were due for a counseling session, so they brought the picture with them—unopened. Their counselor advised them not to open it "until you've made a decision. Otherwise, you'll unlock a Pandora's box of troubles." They discussed the issue during the session, then all the way home in the car. As they pulled into their driveway, Fred slit open the envelope. Trembling with excitement, his first glimpse of the photograph was "a weird moment."

The deformity was severe. The baby's face appeared to have a hole in it from the mouth to the nose. "As gung-ho as I felt," Fred says, "when I saw the photo of the newborn and the extent of the damage, I had my first doubt about myself." Michael pulled the photo out of Fred's hands, took one look, and said: "This baby is adorable, and we are going to love him to pieces." It was an instantaneous and odd role reversal, with Michael certain that "we can take care of this baby, he needs a home, let's go for it!" and Fred suddenly concerned that "we do need new windows."

But the adoption process continued, not always encouragingly. A dentist who looked at the baby's photograph pronounced his condition "pretty severe." Fred went away on a business trip, and Michael used the opportunity to turn an extra bedroom into a nursery, complete with crib and high chair. Fred was afraid it would jinx their chances. "It was a difficult room to be in," he says, "because it was more of a hope than a reality. And it was beginning to feel like a dashed hope." But the hope now had a name—they called the baby Sam—and the process crawled forward, inch by inch.

At the six-month mark, just around the Fourth of July, the INS certified its approval. The adoption agency now had everything it needed to move the process to its conclusion. The requisite papers sped from Seattle to Phnom Penh, and Fred and Michael were told to get ready to fly there the following week. Paperwork snafus in Cambodia, however, put an end to that plan. Instead, that was the week the U.S. government put a freeze on Cambodian adoptions. Under the terms of the freeze, their application was grandfathered, but it was startling to realize that if the adoption agency hadn't sent the papers overseas in time, they would be back at ground zero.

At last everything was cleared for them to go. The flight from Boston to Phnom Penh took 28 hours. Plenty of time for Fred to worry, and he had found plenty to worry about. "Remember," he says; "I'm a reporter. I'm used to downloading a lot of information." Every bit of information loomed in his mind as a potential disaster; every potential disaster seemed a test of his character, which he feared was wanting.

"I worried about how I would feel about our son's cleft lip and palate at the playground when he was next to some other so-called perfect child. I wondered whether I would bond. I worried about attachment disorder."

Fred worried enough for two, and that was fitting, because Michael worried not at all. "Fred was overinformed," Michael says. "He thought only about the horrors: What if this kid doesn't like us or we don't like

him? What if we see him and feel nothing?" Michael "never thought about it. I always believed it would be fine." He pauses. "And of course it was."

Boston–New York–Seattle–Ho Chi Minh City–Phnom Penh. At last the men arrived into the wall of wet heat that is the Cambodian capital's climate. They looked forward to showering, sleeping till the next day, dressing, then being taken to see their son. Instead they were driven directly from the airport to the orphanage, and Sam, now 10 months old, was simply handed to them. "It was a surreal experience," says Fred, "a beautiful moment." His fears and worries evaporated; it was as if they had never existed. Later, when he noticed people staring at Sam, he wondered why—until he remembered Sam had a cleft lip and palate.

Nor was attachment an issue. There they were, surrounded by people—and their son—whose language they did not speak. They could communicate with no one. Yet "Sam came right to us and never looked back," says Fred. "He attached to us instantly."

"He was secure and confident," Michael says. He had been well cared for in the orphanage. He had bonded with his nanny. "Besides," Michael says, "it's his personality: he's a survivor. It takes a special child to survive special needs."

After five more days in Phnom Penh finishing up adoption paperwork, they brought Sam home to Boston and almost immediately to Children's Hospital. "It was awful," says Fred. "We would have liked more time, but we felt we had to begin the process right away." At 10 months, Sam was already old for the surgery.

He underwent three operations in eight months. In the first, doctors closed his palate and implanted ear tubes; the latter gave Sam back much of the 60 percent of his hearing lost through ear infections caused by his underdeveloped Eustachian tubes. The doctors also inserted a device into Sam's mouth to pull his palate together; each day, Fred and Michael had to screw it tight. The second surgery, the most significant of the three, repaired Sam's palate, leaving his lip still open, and the third surgery repaired his lip.

Fred and Michael felt they were living in the hospital.

At home, state-funded intervention began immediately, with physical therapy to overcome problems of malnourishment—a baby with a cleft-palate cannot suck, and Sam weighed less than 13 pounds when he left Cambodia.

Between surgeries and therapies, Fred and Michael took Sam to the beach and to parks and introduced him to numerous cousins—Fred's four siblings live nearby, a strong, loving, very helpful family network. The surgeries began to make a noticeable difference. After a while "only a faint scar" remained, and although Sam will need further surgery in the future, "the heavy lifting has been done," Michael says. The same goes for the malnourishment issue—although "even today, he's a little guy"—and for the speech therapy, which "he will probably be working on for many years."

In the midst of it all, they received information on Sam's origins and a note from his birthmother. "Thank you for taking my son," she wrote. "I have nothing—only two hands to pray for him. Please have him visit me when he is older." Certainly, they will encourage Sam to do so. They even have a fantasy of going back to Cambodia with Sam when he's older, showing him the orphanage, then helping him find his mother. "I would love to meet his mother," says Fred, "if only to thank her."

In January 2001, six months after he arrived in their home, Gabriel and Deveau officially coadopted Sam as parents under Massachusetts

law. It was a highly emotional moment for the two men; Sam just sailed through it.

The same month, they set in motion the adoption of a second child—this time domestic and public, through the Department of Social Services (DSS), with the understanding that "we were open to special-needs kids." Fred's worries about being unable to manage the special-needs experience had fled; "I felt we did it really well," he says, "and I believed we had the capacity to do it again."

They knew the process could take a while—three or four years, they were told—and that was fine, as they wanted a child somewhat younger than Sam. The public adoption process was certainly more thorough and demanding than their international adoption process had been. There was a rigorous homestudy, a requirement to take a five-session training course, and intense coverage of the possible issues with which they might be confronted. "They actually try to scare you," Michael asserts.

In the event, the process took 18 months, and in the summer of 2002, their second son, Jeremiah, came into their lives. He was 13 months at the time—born prematurely to young parents, both Latino, who were unable to take care of him. Fred, typically, had read widely and diagnosed Jeremiah with every possible ailment—but he has none. He had lived with a foster mother since birth and had bonded strongly to her, which helped him bond to Fred and Michael when the time came. His foster mother loved him very much but, at the age of 60, felt she was too old to adopt him. Instead she helped Fred and Michael with the transition and asked to continue to be part of Jeremiah's life. "She'll always be in his life," Michael says firmly. And they will also encourage Jeremiah to find his birth family and reconnect with that part of his history.

"He's a whole different kid," says Fred, "a whole different personality from Sam. It took us a while to see that and honor it." Unlike his older brother, Jeremiah was "fussy, clinging, afraid to go on a swing in the park." The two fathers "had to struggle to see him as a force to be reckoned with" at the same time that they were attending to Sam's natural resentment of his little brother. In due course it all fell into place. The two fathers "started to see moments of the two of them being brothers," says Fred, and the new family of four soon settled into a routine.

Now they say their "tubes are tied," although Fred envisions a day when they're older and can take in kids on a foster basis. For now, however, "we want to make sure that these two have everything we can give them," Michael says: "attention, college, quality time for them to feel loved and wanted." He sees the mandatory "cross-country road trip when they're nine or ten" and admits he'd "like to take them to a Cher concert, maybe for her comeback."

Still, some things have been lost. "Our circle of gay friends is trimmed a bit just because there's no time." They socialize with other parents—mostly straight couples—and while they don't miss "going out clubbing," they do "miss the connection with the gay community, with who we are."

Mostly, however, they feel blessed, as if they hit the perfect moment after all. Says Fred: "The fact that gay men are raising children is not unusual, but the fact that they're setting out to raise children and form families is an important sea change." Fred and Michael caught the crest of the transforming swell. They see themselves as an example that gay men don't have to give up children to live honestly.

Their days are full, and their lives, says Fred, are "on a whole different track. Sometimes I've got a kid on one hip and I'm picking toast up off the floor, and I almost don't recognize me. You lose yourself in the raising of these kids." He hates it when people tell him how "lucky" his children are. "The gift is reciprocal," he insists; "we're the lucky ones."

Beating
Murphy's Law

It took Pericles Rellas and Mitch Edwards two and a half years, 10 county social workers, two private social workers, and a battery of lawyers—including one they buttonholed in a courthouse corridor and hired on the spot—to adopt their children. And it was touch-and-go every step of the way. From bureaucratic snafus to a revolving door of caseworkers to conflicting evaluation reports to disputes between the birthparents themselves, Murphy's Law prevailed, and everything that could go wrong did. Yet every day, Rellas and Edwards shook off the worry, the anger, the tension, and the fear and "strategized how to keep our kids," in Pericles Rellas's phrase. Eventually, to their great relief and with great celebration, they did.

Originally, they had thought about only one child, and their initial aim was to be foster parents. Partners in business as well as in life—Mitch designs "singularly created jewelry" on commission for high-end clients, and Pericles handles the business and administration—they decided on fostering after doing extensive research on how to become parents. Fostering, says Pericles, offered two advantages: it would "give a home to a child who needed one rather than bringing a new life into the world, and while we knew there was no guarantee of adoption as gay dads, we also knew California didn't discriminate against gays for fostering, and that foster parents had the first chance at adopting." Adds Mitch: "We thought it was going to be much easier than it was."

They were interested in fostering an infant, had no restrictions as to color, sex, or religion, but were adamant that the child should be a healthy baby four months or younger. They just didn't feel themselves capable of handling older children or children who might have health problems, especially any problems related to drug use by the mother. So clear were they about these criteria that they agreed that if a call came in and the criteria were met, one of them could decide to say "yes" to a placement even if he couldn't reach the other.

The two men went through the foster parent licensing process and were duly certified. Friends threw them a baby shower, and they soon had on hand all the basics for a full nursery—crib, diapers, bassinet—as well as clothing and the mandatory car seat. Edwards and Rellas sat back to wait.

They were offered an eight-year-old, a six-year-old, a 13-year-old, and while they agonized over these children, they were determined to stick to the criteria they had set. The waiting grew longer. "I think we said 'no' too many times," Mitch mused aloud. After nine months, "we took the bassinet out of the car and put it in the garage," says Pericles, "and that's the day the social worker called with a baby to place."

At the time, Pericles was consulting for an ad agency staffed almost exclusively by women. The call came to him. "We have your four-month-old," the social worker told him, "but there's a catch." Rellas gulped and waited for whatever was coming. "There's a sibling," the social worker went on, "twenty months old. The two are brother and sister, and you must take them both." There was no information on where they came from, what their background was, or how healthy they were; Pericles didn't even know if they had been born drug-addicted, his worst fear.

"Give me five minutes to call Mitch," he told the social worker. Meanwhile, the women in the ad agency office, by now clued in to the fact that something was afoot, had gathered around the phone. They heard Pericles tell Mitch "We've got two" and that he didn't know anything further. They were straining to hear more as the two men figured "we had nothing to lose and everything to gain," Mitch recalls, "and that we should go for it." They heard Mitch call back the social worker and tell her they wanted both babies, and they waited with him while the social worker called the shelter to see if the children were still available. When the phone rang again and Pericles picked it up, the women held their collective breath while the social worker gave him her answer, and when he shouted out "I got my babies!" they screamed and wept and applauded. Pericles suddenly realized he needed another child car seat and had nothing in the way of clothing, furniture, or toys for a toddler. "We'll handle everything," the women told him. Which they did—while Pericles headed out the door to pick up his partner.

But Mitch, who is typically as fastidious as he is punctual, was in his underwear and nowhere near ready. "I realized he was completely

31

numb," says Pericles. The two fathers-to-be talked to one another face to face for the first time about what was about to happen to their lives. They decided, in Mitch's words, that "it would be great." Mitch got dressed, they drove to the store for another car seat, and they headed to the shelter, some 45 minutes out of Los Angeles.

Ashley was playing outside, and Aristotle was in a bouncy chair. Ashley walked up to Pericles, said "Hi," put her arms up, and hugged him. Then she hugged Mitch. Pericles picked up Aristotle and held him. They signed some papers, put their children in the car, picked up dinner at McDonald's, then drove home. "What do we do now?" said Mitch.

Although neither of them had ever changed a diaper in their lives, they at least had been thinking about having an infant; they knew next to nothing about toddlers. That first night, Ashley stayed up till after eleven o'clock just because "we didn't know you had to put her to bed," Mitch says. The next day they bought a book on the subject.

They also noticed signs of serious neglect in Aristotle. "He didn't focus well," says Pericles, "his head was flat in the back, he hardly moved, and he made no noise except when he was hungry, at which point he would scream." His lack of responsiveness made it clear that he had not received sufficient sensory stimulation in infancy, so the two new fathers hired a nanny, stopped working, and devoted themselves full-time to being with their kids, playing with them, and hugging them. By the end of two weeks, says Pericles, "Aristotle was like a normal newborn. He looked around. He loved the Baby Mozart videotape. He was catching up fast." The doctor calculated that he was four to five months behind in development—but gaining—and assured the men that his head would round out in time. It did.

"That whole first month was like a barn-raising," Pericles says, "with everybody dropping everything off"—clothes, toys, ideas. It was a joyous and busy time, and for the children, who had suffered neglect by one parent and the absence of the other, it was an introduction to stability and comfort.

After three months, however, the nightmare began, a tug-of-war involving numerous competing interests, all pressing their varied claims to Ashley and Aristotle, the objects—sometimes it seemed the targets—of dueling public agencies, court orders, and social services reports. Among the players were the children's biological parents, a father in his thirties and a mother still a legal minor, both of whom occasionally operated in the lee of the law and sometimes used parental rights as weapons in their

own disputes. Then there was Social Services, which in this case meant a succession of caseworkers, at least one of them antigay, and none of them, it seemed, in communication with any of the others, so that time after time after time Mitch and Pericles had to start from scratch and educate yet another social worker on their situation. There was the court, which eventually "grew so tired of conflicting reports that the judge appointed her own social workers to investigate us—and was told this was the best foster home she'd ever seen." There were court-appointed lawyers and state-appointed auditors and hearing after hearing after hearing. Each time the men thought adoption was just around the corner, a new wrinkle would suddenly appear—a new demand, a new report, yet another new social worker who had "bad" or "incomplete" notes from the previous social worker.

Mitch and Pericles felt they were walking on eggshells. They were afraid that if they complained about the process or pointed out what they saw as the birthparents' failure to comply with court orders, Social Services, in Mitch's words, "would claim we didn't have the kids' best interests at heart." It was, adds Pericles, as if Social Services was telling them that "our job was to take care of the kids until they figured out what to do with them." That was the one thing Mitch and Pericles were not about to allow. These were their children—of that they were certain—and they had long ago decided, in Pericles' words, "We're going to get them."

But it was hard on them, hard on everyone. Mitch's father had been raised in foster care and was so fearful that the kids might be given back that he steeled himself against becoming attached to them. There were indeed days, his son recalls, when "the possibility of losing them seemed so great, yet every day they spent here was so important." The two determined that "we weren't going to hold back or sell out on them whatever happened, that every day with us would be worth it." Whatever the outcome, they would do for their children all they could do.

In the end—30 months after it began—a fed-up judge determined the case "had been botched so badly she wanted the kids out of the system now," says Mitch. She terminated parental rights the moment an expedited process had approved Edwards and Rellas for the adoption, and at the termination hearing, she told the men: "Bring these kids to my court because I want to do this adoption." The judge had never done an adoption before, but she was immovable in her desire to do this one, and she promised to study up and be ready.

Adoption Day was going to be a big celebration. Mitch's folks flew in from Boston, Pericles' family came from Las Vegas, and friends and even the nanny all showed up at court. It was 9:00 A.M., the appointed time for the proceeding. The judge was ready, the children's court-appointed attorney was ready, and the mother's attorney was ready; all that was needed was the Rellas-Edwards attorney—who, inexplicably, failed to show up. Pericles got on the phone and called everywhere—to no avail. At 9:30, there was talk of rescheduling, but Pericles and Mitch insisted they were "not leaving without adopting these children."

"I'll fire the lawyer and represent myself," Mitch said. You can't, he was told.

"I'll find an attorncy," Pericles said. After all, it was a courthouse. He turned around, and there was Paul. "You don't know me," Pericles said to the total stranger in the courthouse hallway, "but I would like to hire you to represent us so we can adopt our children. Right now. My entire family is here. I'll pay you a thousand dollars if you do this." The startled lawyer blanched, stammered, shrugged, then smiled. "I'll be happy to do it," said Paul, "and I'll do it for free." He turned and looked at the assembled family members. "Where's your wife?" he asked. "Paul," said Pericles, "you have no idea what you've gotten into. I have a partner." As the light dawned, Paul smiled again. "That's great," he said.

"Actually," Paul went on as he quickly scanned the paperwork, "you have no idea what *you've* gotten into. I've never done this before."

"Neither have we," Pericles replied. "And neither has the judge."

Nevertheless, in August 2001, two and a half years after Ashley and Aristotle came to live with Mitch and Pericles, they legally became Ashley and Aristotle Edwards-Rellas. Little Aristotle never really had any idea the whole process was happening, says Mitch, but Ashley had a sense of it and was upset by all the social workers going in and out of the house. Her fathers tell her that she and her brother had a mommy and daddy who loved them very much but couldn't take care of them, so they waited for the best parents to come and take care of them, "and we showed up." The story, they hope, provides a sense that the children were loved before, are loved now, and will be loved forever. What is certain is that Ashley loves to hear the story.

The Edwards-Rellas family lives in a quintessential California suburb of "half-acre lots, streetlamps, and sidewalks," says Mitch. The men didn't want to raise the kids in an exclusive enclave like Bel Air, nor in a gay "ghetto" like West Hollywood, but in a "neighborhood that's nothing in particular." The two maintain an office in Beverly Hills but spend time in their home office as well. "We're here when they get home," says Mitch. "Somebody is always here for them." The children enjoy a double ethnic tradition—Jewish and Greek—are doted on by both sets of grandparents, and have an array of aunts, uncles, and cousins.

The children call Mitch Daddy and Pericles Princess. Pericles tells why: "When they first came, I would always call Ashley 'my little princess,' and after a month or so, she pointed at me and said 'Princess.' The more I protested, the more she did it. Then Mitch started calling me that, and now everybody calls me Princess."

They think the name is one reason they have never confronted homophobia with the kids. "We are outed everywhere because I am called 'Princess,'" Pericles asserts. "Usually, two men with two kids makes people think: 'You left the wives home tonight.' But this outs us. And people love it. They embrace us"—although he attributes much of the family attraction to the fact that his kids are "great, personable, precocious."

They are lucky, they think, that "everybody is so open here in Los Angeles," as Mitch puts it. "We're visible," he says. When he enrolled the children in a private school, he raised the fact of their having two fathers. Said the principal: "We have kids here from 20 countries and eight religions. All we care about is that you be decent people."

They are decent people with two happy, healthy children. That fact alone makes what they went through to adopt the children "worth every bit of it," says Mitch. Ashley and Aristotle are very close; they have never been separated. Now they never have to be—not from each other, and not from their fathers.

The People Who Didn't
Give Up

Emmy swam out like a little dolphin with her eyes open," says Rick Shaver of the moment of his daughter's birth. Rick was holding the birthmother's legs, and Lee Melahn, his partner and Emmy's other father, cut the cord, and "it was incredible." Shaver's voice begins to crack with emotion. "A nurse took Emmy over to a little heating table, and I said, 'Can I touch her?' And the nurse said, 'Of course, she's your daughter.' And I began to blubber—and kept it up for the next two hours." Shaver blubbers as he recalls it. "This is a door that as a gay man I had closed many years before; having it open was a miracle."

But it had taken a lot to realize the miracle and pry the door open.

Rick Shaver and Lee Melahn have been together since 1979. They are professional partners as well as life partners, owners of Shaver-Melahn Studios, a multidiscipline design firm. They had been a couple for a decade when Lee first brought up the subject of children, but Rick wasn't interested. "Back then, I couldn't even figure out why you would *want* to have a child."

Then Rick's mother became ill, and he headed home to Georgia to care for her. "I reconnected with my family on a daily basis more than I had in twenty years, and it made me yearn to have a family of my own." So when Rick returned to New York after his mother's death, he announced to Lee that he was now ready to bring a child into their lives. This time, Lee was hesitant. "I was in my mid-forties," Lee says. "I didn't know whether I felt comfortable about being a parent; I thought I would be too old." In time, Rick reconvinced him. "My hesitation yielded to my desire to have a child," Lee says simply. The question then became: where to start?

Around the end of 1993, uncertainly but "very actively," Shaver and Melahn began to pursue the idea of adopting a child. The pursuit would take them down a number of what Lee calls "wrong avenues." The starting-point for their journey was "a lot of disinformation," much of it from gay-centered community organizations. "Everything was very negative," Rick says. "We were told how difficult this was all going to be, were told not to go through normal channels, that we should expect trouble." They were also advised they would probably only be able to adopt an older child or a child who didn't meet their desired criteria, whatever those criteria might be. It was as if they were doused with reality before they had a chance to dip their toes in the water. It was a dispiriting beginning.

Since they knew that as two middle-aged men they didn't fit the demographics for public adoption, their focus was on a private, open adoption. They found a lawyer through New York's Lesbian and Gay Community Services Center, a crossroads for gay organizations, institutions, and community programs at the epicenter of the city's Greenwich Village. The lawyer eventually hooked them up with an individual who promised "Whatever you want, I can get for you."

"We talked to this guy a lot," says Lee, "and every time we talked, his fee went up. It was clear that he was brokering babies." Rick found dealing with him "uncomfortable" at best and thought it "smacked of being illegal" at worst. "Everyone has moments of discouragement," says Lee. "We were very discouraged."

Then Rick began work on an interior decoration project with a married couple who had a two-year-old son. At their apartment one day, he remarked to the mother not just how adorable her son was but how closely he resembled her husband. "That's funny," said the client. "Our son is adopted." Rick blushed, stammered, and prayed for the floor to open beneath him. His client wasn't embarrassed, however. In fact, she was downright eager to share the details of her family's adoption process. She also recommended the lawyer who had helped make it possible—Suzanne Nichols, an adoption specialist with offices in a suburb of New York. Rick and Lee met with Nichols and liked her. "The only people who end up without a baby," she told them, "are the people who give up." It became their mantra. Says Shaver: "Every time I confronted a problem in the process, Suzanne would repeat this to us, and we listened to her—thank God."

By this time "we had been spinning our wheels for eight or nine months," Shaver says. They still had a long way to go, but at least now they felt they had help they could rely on. They also felt a bit like pioneers.

Nichols had never before dealt with two gay men in an adoption situation, and Rick and Lee were determined to go through the process "as a gay couple," in Rick's phrase, "with no dissembling, with everything above board." It meant, Lee adds, that "we were all blazing a new trail."

Nichols's recommendation was that they follow the normal route for private adoption: advertise in newspapers, deal directly with the birthmothers who respond, come to an understanding, be involved during the pregnancy and present at the birth. "She felt confident; we felt skeptical," Rick says.

The recommended advertising blitz ran for two weeks, concentrating on newspapers in small towns or college towns—locales likely to contain women who did not want to have abortions—and in states where the laws would be favorable to gay adoption. It yielded a number of leads, the most promising of which was a woman in Tennessee who was already in her second trimester of pregnancy. They liked her, and she liked them, and they worked with her for four full months, paying the legal limit on her living and medical expenses. But two weeks before she was due to give birth, she stopped taking their calls. It was a devastating blow for Shaver and Melahn. The spent money was the least painful element of the loss. "I thought: we cannot get past this," says Lee. "I thought: this will not happen. But Rick reminded me of what Suzanne said about giving up, and we got back on the horse and put another ad in the papers."

The two later learned that pressure from her family had persuaded the Tennessee birthmother to keep her baby. It taught Shaver and Melahn an important lesson—that "it's not enough just to convince the birthmother," says Lee; rather, "you're dealing with a whole network of people"—family, friends, and who knows who else who may have influence over the pregnant woman.

For the new ad blitz, they contravened their lawyer's advice in one key respect. Nichols had told them that the one paper they most certainly should *not* advertise in was *USA Today*. "You'll just get hate calls," she told them. They went ahead and placed an ad there anyway, then steeled themselves for the bigotry. It was the winter of 1996, Rick recalls. "There were blizzards once a week, and I was locked in, watching the snow and waiting for the phone to ring." There *were* hate calls, but surprisingly few, and not just hate calls but serious discussions as well. One discussion connected them to a woman from a Plains state. She was in the first trimester of her pregnancy and in a relationship that was not working; she wanted out of the relationship and out of the state. It sounded good, but Shaver and Melahn were wary and didn't want to raise their hopes too high. Their lawyer had advised them to create a relationship with the woman, to make her feel comfortable, and to "convince her that we would be good parents." As they now well knew, you couldn't always be certain of an individual's circumstances or motivations, not to mention the fact that both her circumstances and her motivations could change. Obviously, they had to tread carefully.

Rick took on the task of being her major interlocutor. "We just chatted. As a gay boy who had always had close girlfriends, I found it easy to engage with her about her life and our lives." On the other hand, "I had to call her when her boyfriend was working, so I often felt like I was dating a married woman." Lee kept reminding Rick—and himself—that they must never be judgmental. That was easy with this woman. Both men found her bright and intelligent, with realistic and closely reasoned rationales for her actions.

Their lawyer was eager to move the birthmother to a state where the laws were more favorable to adoptive parents. The mother agreed, so Nichols's office found an adoption agency in another state, and Shaver and Melahn paid moving expenses and the agency fee for medical, counseling, and other services. Things were going well. They had not yet met the birthmother in person, but they talked with her daily, and all three had exchanged photos. What's more, the birthfather had signed the legal document relinquishing his rights to the child.

The birthmother was now in her second trimester, with everything ticking along smoothly, and then suddenly, says Rick, "she stopped answering or returning our calls." The reason? Nichols learned from the agency that the birthmother's own family had "hit the roof" when they heard the baby would be adopted by gay men. Once again "the network" had stepped in to wreak havoc with their lives. It felt "like a kick in the stomach," says Rick, and for a while "we languished."

They turned their attention to moving into a new apartment and redoing it from top to bottom. It was closer to their studio, and they wanted to make it ready for a child. Then they tried another ad blitz and had "a short episode" with a woman who had a serious drug problem. They also dabbled with the idea of surrogacy and considered international adoption. "We were desperate," says Rick, "and we were battle weary. We knocked on every door we could find."

The phone call from their Plains-state birthmother was a bolt from the blue. Yes, she had been dissuaded from letting gay men adopt her child and had been working recently with a straight couple the agency had found for her. But she didn't like the straight couple; in particular, she didn't like the woman. It's not uncommon for birthmothers to prefer gay men as adoptive parents rather than a woman who might be seen as a replacement, even a rival. This birthmother was now seven and a half months pregnant and again wanted Shaver and Melahn to adopt her child.

The two were ecstatic but nervous. If once burned is twice shy, twice burned is downright withdrawn. "Stay in touch with her," advised their lawyer, "but go about your lives." They took a SkyTel beeper on vacation with them and panicked when they got a message saying labor had begun. It was a false labor, but they raced home anyway and picked up the pace on their apartment reconstruction.

The birthmother convinced the doctor to induce labor and wanted Rick and Lee there. On the flight out, Rick realized that "there" meant in the delivery room; "I am so squeamish I didn't think I could do it." What's more, it was a Methodist hospital, and he imagined people "thumping Bibles at us." He was wrong on both counts. People "treated us like celebrities," and their meeting with the birthmother, says Lee, was "very special and very precious." What's more, "she looked like Rick's sister." Instantly the two were active participants in the whole hospital process. When labor was induced at 6:00 the following morning, they gave the mother back rubs and helped when the contractions came, and when at 11:00 A.M. the doctor said "We're gonna go," they were right there and not one whit squeamish when their daughter "swam out like a little dolphin with her eyes open."

They couldn't take Emmy home that night, and they found that hard. The next day, the birthmother asked to see and hold the tiny, six-pound baby. With tears in her eyes, she assured them she was fine. "I prepared myself for this," she said. "This is your child." She signed the papers relinquishing her rights to Emmy, and she went home.

The new Shaver-Melahn family of three had to remain in town for 11 days for all the paperwork to be completed. They had found a bed-and-breakfast run by a lesbian couple who were almost as excited about the birth as they were. When the new fathers brought Emmy to the bed-and-breakfast, a basket of toys awaited her. When they flew home with her to New York, the stewardesses plied them with champagne. In the little town in upstate New York where Rick and Lee have spent weekends since the mid-1980s, the locals surprised them with a baby shower and filled their house with balloons. "This was eye-opening," says Lee. "You harbor such fears, and yet people have been so open and embracing."

Emmy's birth did necessitate one rather tricky maneuver. While their siblings and extended family members all knew they were gay, neither Rick nor Lee had ever come out to their remaining parents—Rick's father and Lee's mother. It was time. In both cases, there were a couple of rough hours as the two wrestled with acceptance. Both eventually came around. They adore their granddaughter, as do the cousins, uncles, and aunts of her extended family.

With her fathers, Emmy divides her time between city and country and is at home in both. Her fathers feel that she "completes" them; she makes them a family and rounds out their happiness.

Safely Home

Visualize this situation," says Sam Cruz, father of Daelyon (pronounced Day-Lon). "You're a small child, and someone knocks in the middle of the night and takes you away to somewhere you've never been and to someone you don't know. You lose everything, and everything changes for the worse. My home was number eleven for Daelyon, and he was six years old." Cruz's voice still tightens with sorrow and anger when he talks about it, when he imagines what his son went through and thinks about "how this had shaped him." What is done to a child over a period of years, especially the early years, takes time to undo. "It's a long road," says Cruz.

Sam Cruz is a Bronx boy with a New England accent. The middle child of a close-knit family of Puerto Rican origin, he was born in New York, lived briefly in Puerto Rico—he is fluent in Spanish as well as English—and did most of his growing up in Meriden, Connecticut. He was never in the closet. He had his first boyfriend early in high school and remembers attending the very first fundraiser for Gay Men's Health Crisis at Madison Square Garden in New York. The gay community filled the Garden—16,000 strong. "It was a turning point for me," Cruz acknowledges, an important stage in his development. What he calls "the next step" was "thinking about having a family."

It made sense. His parents were loving, protective, traditional, committed to spending time with their six children. "That was comfortable," Cruz says; "that felt like what I wanted to do."

In his early twenties, he broached the idea with his partner, but the partner wasn't interested. When they separated—Cruz was 26—he "didn't want to start a family in the throes of loss," so he told himself to wait a year. While he waited, his mother became ill with breast cancer—another reason to put his own life on hold.

In 1995, Sam Cruz was 30, and the state of Connecticut was desperate for foster parents. It's when Sam "really started to get things together." He attended an open house at a gay bookstore in a tiny old mill town on the Farmington River, where half a dozen people showed up to hear a representative of the sponsoring agency, herself a lesbian, talk about the planned legislative changes that would enable gay couples and singles to foster and then adopt children. A gay couple who had just completed an adoption was on tap as living proof. "It became solid in my mind that this could happen," Cruz says. That was November. In March of the following year, Cruz's mother died—slowly, painfully, and too young. His father had died four years previously. The deaths were reminders of "how precious life is and how short. If I wanted to do this, it was clear I should get off my butt and get moving."

Cruz went about the task methodically. He turned his guest room into a child's room, fixed up his house, built up his savings. He had a homestudy done and undertook a 14-week training course in foster parenting with Connecticut's Department of Children and Families (DCF). He went to counseling to be sure he would be a good parent and that his penchant for being in control would not be passed on as a father, "especially to kids who might be damaged from years of trouble." He studied Hold Therapy, a technique often used to counteract attachment issues, and read a lot on child psychology, seeking to understand a child's point of view.

When DCF called, they asked him to "please go visit" a five-year-old—call him Tommy—at the state hospital. "Had I known more of his history," Cruz says, "I might not have visited, but I didn't know I could say no." In fact, he knew little. He had no idea how disturbed Tommy was—with severe attention deficit and hyperactivity disorder, bipolarity, and probably schizophrenia; he didn't even know whether an attention span of 60 seconds maximum was normal or abnormal for a five-year-old. After several visits, an overnight, and a weekend, Tommy moved in with Sam, for what Cruz would describe as "the longest six months of my life."

Tommy couldn't sleep, grew angry, screamed obscenities for an hour at a time. When he threw a tantrum at the mall, Sam did Hold Therapy "to try to keep him from banging his head on the concrete floor." Other shoppers gave them a wide berth. When a security guard approached, Sam grew nervous; after all, he carried no ID saying he was responsible for Tommy, and although Tommy was also Latino, he was darker skinned than Sam—not recognizable as a relative. Finally, after being held for 20 minutes, Tommy calmed down.

"It was hard to believe that a five-year-old could be that damaged," Cruz says. He had been severely abused by a schizophrenic mother who alternated between doting on him excessively and beating him. He had seen his mother being battered by men. And she had probably used heroin or cocaine during her pregnancy. Tommy himself was never without a daily dose of Thorazine and other drugs. He went to special school and a special extended-day facility, and there were home visits by DCF social workers, but in the whole apparatus of child care, there was nothing anyone could give Sam to help Tommy.

He made it up as he went along, and he began to make a difference. "By working out a really strict pattern for every day and not deviating, I was able to get him to go to bed on time, dress himself, do the necessities," Cruz says. "It was success at some level. And he was starting to reveal his feelings. He listened to a message on the machine from his mother, and it was the first time I saw him cry."

Tommy went back to his mother after six months with Sam. She had "started to get her life together," although it didn't last. In time, Tommy was again removed from her care and institutionalized—"probably forever," Sam says. Tommy "taught me a lot—that no matter how damaged a child is, there's a human being there somewhere. And no matter how hard it is to reach them, it's so rewarding." But it is "not a linear process. You start, stop, go back, go forward. It's a human being, not a building. From Tommy I learned patience—and that I could endure a lot."

Four months later, a 13-year-old we'll call Luis came to live with Sam and showed him "the other end of the scale." Nine years old when he had witnessed his stepfather's suicide, Luis was the oldest of four children of a woman who was in and out of depression, on and off drugs. He had been hospitalized at 12 and was eager to be in a home. "Charming, intelligent, a wonderful boy," Sam says of Luis, who went from a psychiatric hospital to being an A/B student at a regular middle school. He stayed with Sam for nearly a year before being placed with his grandparents.

Sam was opposed to the placement. He thought it was a bad idea for Luis, and he said as much in letters he "wrote to everyone that would listen." He argued that Luis needed separation from his mother and a group home where he would find structure. But as a foster parent, Sam had no rights. Luis returned to his grandparents and has since been in and out of state care.

Sam was angry. He was also weary. He told DCF he "didn't want to see another child for six months." But two months later, on a Friday in July 1999, DCF called with an emergency situation: A kid had been pulled from a foster home after 10 months because of physical abuse; he needed a safe place right away. Sam said he would have to think about it. On Tuesday he said okay, "but for no more than six months." DCF assured him that the child's mother was "on track" and would be ready to have him back by then. Daelyon moved in that Friday, July 15, 1999.

He was six, African-American, and when Sam first visited him in temporary foster care, he thought he might have another Tommy on his hands. Daelyon was "jumping around, beating up the inflatables" in the playroom. It turned out that pro wrestling was the major entertainment enjoyed by the foster family Daelyon had been with; it was the only play he knew.

That foster family had more to answer for. "Daelyon's hair was matted," Cruz says, "his skin was ashy, his shorts were too big, and he wore black dress socks with sneakers that didn't fit. It was evident that attention had not been paid, and it tugged at my heart. All his possessions were in a paper bag, and they didn't fill the bag." Sam took him home and took a week off, spending time with the boy, shopping for him, setting up his room.

Daelyon was not quick to attach. He was not trusting. He stayed at a distance. Sam found him a daycare situation for the rest of the summer, then enrolled him in school. He was old enough for the second grade, but he couldn't read, so he was assigned to special education. Sam and Daelyon set a goal: that Daelyon would work his way out of special ed by middle school. "I read to him every night," Sam says, "then had him read a little. He also got a lot of help at school, and I was very involved in that."

Daelyon had some behavior problems, too. He routinely got into fights with other kids. "He was incredibly angry," Cruz says. "Any little thing might set him off."

The first year was tough. The visits from his mother confused Daelyon, especially when she dropped out of his life entirely after a visit. Sometimes she would arrive stoned, and Daelyon had to witness the police escorting her away. Visits to his father in prison elicited paternal promises that were never fulfilled. Daelyon himself had to be kept busy all the time with a lineup of after-school activities. Sam needed all his training and experience to manage the situation—with help from the caseworker and a therapist.

It took a year before Daelyon could refer to Sam as Dad—and Sam had to ask for it. "We sat down, and I told him I felt I deserved the respect of being called Dad. I could tell that Daelyon had mixed feelings."

"Sometimes I want to, but I forget," Daelyon said. His birthfather remained a dashing figure to Daelyon and was certainly a loving one. To call Sam Dad would require letting go of that—at least to some extent. Sam argued that Daelyon "can have us both." It worked. Daelyon "called me Sam one more time and never since."

Also around that time, DCF began proceedings to terminate the parental rights of Daelyon's birthparents so Sam could adopt him. It took 18 months. The court had little trouble finding Daelyon's mother incapable of caring for her son, but his father, as the judge put it, "was not neglectful, just in jail. I would prefer it," the judge told Sam and his lawyer, "if you could get him to give up his rights voluntarily."

They met alone, without lawyers, over a glass divider pocked with holes, and "we both negotiated for our son.

"It was bizarre," says Sam. "I tried to convince him that I would be a good father, that I didn't begrudge him his love of his son, that I wanted to do what was best for Daelyon."

Daelyon's birthfather, in turn, conceded that he had "screwed up" his life. "But I love my son," he said, "and I don't want to lose him."

In the end, they agreed that Sam would voluntarily allow the father to see Daelyon and that the father would give up his rights unconditionally. It was "an incredible experience," Sam says. On July 3, 2001, just shy of two years after Daelyon came to him, Sam became his father.

They make a small but powerful family. Daelyon, who has tested above average for intelligence, beat his goal of getting out of special ed by a year; father and son then set their sights on the honor roll. He plays football and has lots of friends, including a best friend who is also African-American. He has known since early on—since he first asked about having a mother—that his father is gay and that there might someday be another dad. Father and son routinely participate in gay Family Week in Provincetown, Massachusetts, attend picnics and potlucks of the gay network, and go to conferences for gay teenagers where Sam volunteers.

As the black son of a gay Latino man, even in a town that is integrated on many levels, Daelyon has a head start in understanding bigotry. When he told his best pal, Isaiah, that his father was gay, Isaiah said he wasn't sure his parents would let him come to Daelyon's house anymore. Tearfully, Daelyon reported this to Sam. "I explained to him that what Isaiah feared was indeed possible, but I would do all I could to preserve their friendship," Sam says. "Daelyon admires Martin Luther King very much, so I talked about King. I said the best we can do is be who we are, be proud of it, and love others unconditionally, for love was the only way to beat hatred. He went to bed okay with that."

When Isaiah told his parents, their response was clear. "Good," they said. "We want you to grow up knowing that there are many kinds of families."

Maybe the toughest thing was when Sam and Daelyon moved in the summer of 2001. Sam wanted to get Daelyon off their busy street into a neighborhood with lots of space and lots of kids. He also wanted the move itself to be a positive experience, so he involved Daelyon in all the house-hunting. But Daelyon still seemed worried. "Can I take my radio?" he would ask. "What about my toy box? Can I take it with me? Can I take my posters?" It finally dawned on Sam "that my concept of moving had always been to a better place—with all the old stuff plus more. Daelyon's concept of moving was to go to a scary unknown and lose everything."

Sam reassured Daelyon but cried himself to sleep that night thinking about what his son had suffered. In the end, the move turned out to be "great"—great neighborhood, great school, great kids. The road is still long, but it seems to have brought father and son home safely.

A Surrogate's Gift

I don't worry too much about the psychology of it," says David, who with his partner, Don, is the father of twins.* "There are many, many things that children resent their parents for, and we might go through the stage of our kids resenting us for being gay. But if it is not this, it will be something else. The only answer is unconditional love. And our two babies are loved more than any could be."

The two babies who are the focus of this statement—and of the unconditional love—were born through a process of gestational surrogacy.

*To protect their privacy, David and Don have chosen to be identified by first names only.

They are the biological offspring of David and an anonymous egg donor and were carried and delivered by a gestational surrogate.

It sounds simple, but of course it wasn't. Along the way there were obstacles, challenges, doubts, lawyers with contracts, doctors with test tubes, biological cycles to be meshed and airline schedules to be coordinated, fees and expenses to be paid. Lots of fees and expenses, in fact. What made it all particularly thorny—and what makes the resulting family such a formidable achievement—is that these fathers and their children live in Arkansas, a part of the country where a long tradition of religious fundamentalism still echoes in many aspects of life. It is a place where it is often not easy to be gay—much less a gay couple—so to be the only gay dads in their state to have achieved fatherhood through surrogacy, as Don and David are pretty sure they are, seems gutsy indeed.

Both men come by it naturally. David grew up in the state. His parents divorced, and he rarely saw his father, but his mother had strong religious views that would eventually clash significantly with the reality of David's sexuality. David put off the reality for a while; he married right out of college but divorced after three years. Coming out was no picnic. It was "rough going" with his mother. Homosexuality, she preached to him, was "an abomination," "a choice," and something that could be "healed"—the usual fire-and-brimstone nonsense.

Even worse than his mother's discomfort, however, as she tried to reconcile her love for her son with her religious beliefs, was David's own difficulty in dealing with the notion that he wouldn't be a father. "Growing up, I had always envisioned myself becoming a father. It was very much a part of my identity. So when I came out, I really had a difficult time with the notion that I wouldn't be a father." In 1987, however, David saw a cover story in the *Advocate* about gay men becoming fathers; one of the options discussed in the story was surrogacy. The idea was planted in his mind.

What with law school, starting a career, and being involved in a relationship, however, the idea stayed on the back burner till David was in his early thirties and decided to pursue it actively. He was stopped at just about every turn. "There were incredible obstacles for gay men at that time," he says, "incredible difficulties placed in their way. You had to travel all over the country to find a surrogate agency willing to work with gays, or to find doctors who wouldn't discriminate." At one point, in fact, David had hooked up with an agency and connected with a surrogate. "Don't tell the doctor you're working with a gay man," the agency warned the surrogate. Sure enough, when the doctor learned that the sperm donor was gay, he left the surrogate on the examining table and walked out of the room.

David was 35 and Don 30 when they met in 1996. Don was raised Southern Baptist in the Deep South, not very distant in spiritual terms from David's childhood environment. When he was thinking about moving to Arkansas, a friend there fixed him up with David, and that decided him. He got into real estate after the two had a miserable experience buying their home; he decided that "nobody else should have to go through this."

The topic of children came up "early in the relationship," when David made it clear "that if we were to become partners in life, it was important for me to have children." Don felt the same. "We were both excited about the idea," he says. In the face of what David described as "a drive— a longing—for biological offspring," their thinking consistently focused on surrogacy as the "preferred route." But they decided to wait a year be-

fore doing anything "to ensure that our relationship was stable and to give us some time together."

At the end of the year, they logged onto the Internet and starting advertising for women who might be interested in serving as surrogates. Internet searching seemed a good idea in light of David's unpleasant past experiences with surrogacy agencies, but the blind, scattershot searches seemed only to yield "some strange people," in Don's phrase.

One day while surfing the Net, however, they found the site for Growing Generations, the innovative gay and lesbian–owned surrogacy agency based in Los Angeles. It seemed too good to be true—gay people with children "whose whole purpose," David says, "was to work with other gay people and help them become parents." They flew out there to see for themselves and met with the founder, Gail Taylor, and with Will Halm, the family law attorney who chairs Growing Generations. To David, a veteran of surrogacy attempts that had been discriminatory and dismissive failures, the "difference in the whole environment" was striking. Clearly, for gay men seeking to be parents through surrogacy, things had changed—big-time. Don and David went through the Growing Generations interview, the medical screening, the application process, and the background reports, and, says Don, "we were accepted."

One bonus of dealing with Growing Generations was immediately evident: the agency handled all the advertising for surrogates *and* screened out the crazies. But it also quickly became clear that it was going to take time to match the profile David and Don had compiled with the right surrogate profile. These profiles comprised not just bald facts and figures but also a checklist of how much contact the parties wanted, what they saw as each other's future role in their lives, views on actions to be taken if birth defects were detected, and willingness to accept twins. The two men sat back and waited.

The wait was nine months long—the gestation period of a human being. "We have matched you with a surrogate," Gail Taylor announced to the two men, then told them about her: a lesbian, surprisingly, who had conceived her own child through artificial insemination by a gay man and now wanted to return the favor by becoming a surrogate to gay men. David and Don phoned her and "hit it off," in Don's words. They then flew the surrogate and her partner to Los Angeles and met them there for a face-to-face meeting. That too "went well."

Then came what David calls "the agonizing part": choosing the egg donor. "You have to look at everything," he goes on: "health issues, intellect, appearance, everything you can learn about the person." They combed through notebooks full of potential donors, ranked their first and second choices, then changed their minds and asked if there wasn't one more notebook to look through. "It was a gut feeling," David says. "We saw her in the book, and she just popped out." He added: "We felt her physical characteristics were appealing, she seemed very smart and creative, well adjusted, stable, so many talents and features." David pauses. "And mostly it was the warmth that we sensed in her."

Once all the basic choices were made, lawyers got into the act. "Each side has its lawyer," says Don. "You start with the model worked out from the matched profiles. Then you negotiate up from there"—compensation, contingencies, insurance, maternity clothes allowance, childcare expenses while the surrogate attends medical appointments. Next it was the turn of the doctors. The donor was given a course of medication to stimulate her ovaries. At the same time, the reproductive cycles of both donor and surrogate were monitored so that doctors could ensure as much as possible that the surrogate would receive a freshly fertilized embryo at the optimal moment. With the egg donor in one location, the surrogate in another, and Don and David in yet a third, this coordination was no easy task.

In due course the women's cycles were in sync, and a date was set for the fertilization. On the projected day, however, the egg donor unaccountably got her period, which promptly put an end to attempt number one. It was "very stressful," says Don. But eventually the cycles were back on course, and the parties converged—without meeting face-to-face—on a fertility clinic in Los Angeles. In one room, David supplied a semen sample—the plan was that he would be the biological father of a first child and Don the father of a possible second child—while in another room, doctors were taking eggs from the egg donor. The eggs were fertilized in vitro, and three days later, after giving the embryonic cells time to divide and multiply, the surrogate arrived for implantation.

"The surrogate is required to have bed rest for two days after the implantation procedure," Don explains, "and we were so nervous and scared we wouldn't let her out of bed. We watched movies together for two days." It was "nerve-wracking," he adds, "because the pregnancy usually doesn't take the first time."

Emotionally ready for a negative result, Don and David flew home and prepared to wait 11 days. It was the Christmas season, and as Don was hanging the Christmas stockings one evening, some impulse led him to hang two extras. "I had a feeling it would be twins," he recalls.

The implantation had worked; David and Don got the news that their surrogate was pregnant. With that as a Christmas gift, they enjoyed an especially happy holiday season. The next month, they headed to Houston, the surrogate's hometown, for her ultrasound exam. That's when they learned that Don's two "extra" stockings were prophetic: It was twins all right—"a shock," says David, but a happy one. They shifted gears mentally and plunged into involvement in the surrogate's pregnancy—including being on-the-spot in Houston for every single one of her scheduled doctor visits. It meant taking considerable time off work, and that in turn meant that David, at least, felt he had to let his law partners in on the news about his impending fatherhood. Don, on the other hand, didn't want anyone to know, lest the telling "jinx it." Both men worried about the extra risks of a multiple pregnancy, talked every night to the surrogate, and kept a pregnancy journal. When their surrogate got an okay from the doctor to vacation in Disney World, the men worried every moment till she returned home safely.

It was the third trimester—right around Eastertime—before David told his mother. He did so by putting two pairs of booties—one pink, one blue—in an Easter egg for her. She got it right away, and she was thrilled—these would be her first grandchildren. Her excitement quickly translated into a realization that she could no longer be closeted about her son, his partner, and their life together. Suddenly, she just let it all go—and found she had no trouble telling her friends both that her son was gay and that she was to be a grandmother. As to his seldom seen father, David came out to him and told him about the twins at the same time, and he too has been accepting.

Don, however, had determined to wait until the babies were born before telling his parents, but in the end events overtook his carefully laid out plan. For one thing, the twins came six weeks early. David and Don got a call that the surrogate's water had broken and that she was going in for a C-section. By the time the men arrived at the hospital, their children were already a couple of hours old. Aidan had been born first and easily, but Alaina fought the emergence, kicking and screaming the whole way—which is exactly what their personalities are like today, their fathers say. Both babies went immediately into the intensive care unit (ICU), but the next day their fathers had a chance to hold them as well as look at them. Alaina was out of the ICU after three days, but Aidan needed a longer stay. At less than two weeks old, both came home.

The "main thing" about twins, says David, "is that it was so hard. They did not have the same schedule, we never slept, and Aidan was on the heart monitor"—for apnea, not uncommon in the case of twins. For the first three months, David and Don alternated every other day at work so that one of them was always home. Thanks to the twins having been born in Texas, a state where some courts allow second parent and same-sex adoption, Don was able to prove he was adopting and to get family leave. David just says his law partners were "really good about it." As to Don's having missed out on the chance to be a biological father, he shrugs it off. "I never even think about it," he says. "These are my kids, and that's all there is to it."

The day Don's parents arrived to see the babies was the day they finally learned he was gay. They learned it from David's mother. She was at home when Don's parents arrived to see the twins for the first time; David, Don, and the babies were at the pediatrician. David's mother opened the door to Don's folks, welcomed them to the house, and told them about the routine doctor visit. The three "in-laws," who had never met, began to chat. "Yes," David's mother said at one point during the conversation, "I had a difficult time when David told me he was gay, but I love him just the same. And we're so glad that he found Don; we love him just like he's part of our family." Don's parents survived the jolt, have adjusted well, and are Maw-Maw and Paw-Paw to the twins. But other family members continue to fear that Don is damned.

Somewhat to their surprise, David and Don have enjoyed a "mostly positive response" from the public they interact with. "Two men with twins is a real attention-getter," says David. Their own neighborhood is heavily fundamentalist, and the men feel they are providing something of an education to their neighbors. "A few people have said that 'other' neighbors have a problem with us but they do not," David says. "I think people will have to do some soul-searching. It is much harder to express your bigotry in the face of children, and I think they will have to come to grips with the fact that our family is not much different from theirs."

The coming-to-grips moves by inches, but it moves. As new fathers, David and Don applied for membership in the local Mothers of Twins Club. Their application was met with some nervousness and, eventually, with rejection. They were told they could subscribe to the newsletter and attend the garage sale, but that was it; they wouldn't even be allowed to come to the Mothers of Twins' events for fathers. Two and a half years later, David got a call from a new Mother of Twins inviting them to a club event. "It's wrong," the woman told David. "Those people who turned you down should go jump in the lake."

Don and David are careful to "lay the groundwork of two dads" every time they take the twins into a new setting. "We don't want teachers in daycare taking out their frustrations on babies because they don't like gays," says Don. They are also adamant that "we don't want only one person recognized as the father. As the twins get older, everyone needs to be aware they have two dads, so they aren't asked awkward questions like 'Where's your mommy?' "

The twins have no mommy. It's as simple as that. A surrogate carried them and "will always have a special place" in the family's life, David says. She performed an essential function that their fathers were simply incapable of performing, but the family is two children and two fathers.

Ordinary People

Huntington, Long Island, may be the American suburban town at its best. Diverse, tolerant, with a vibrant downtown and a wide variety of living and working environments, Huntington's designation by the Chamber of Commerce as an "all-American city" would surprise no one.

By the same token, Huntington's Cooper family may be the American suburban family at its best. A stay-at-home parent deeply involved in the community and the children's school, a breadwinner parent who also coaches soccer and is politically active, and five children—three girls, two of them twins, and two boys—with nine years separating the youngest from the oldest: the Coopers are about as normal, as ordinary a family as you can get. In a way, it is their very ordinariness that is so notable.

Jon Cooper was born on Long Island and has lived there all his life. Rob is Cuban born and moved with members of his family to Europe in the mid-1960s, then to the United States in 1979. The two met at a discotheque on the north shore of the Island, where Jon had returned, after college and a bit of "bumming around the country," to run his family's biotechnology manufacturing business. Their meeting sparked "love at first sight," says Jon, and the two moved in together almost at once. Jon was successful in bringing new growth to the family business, one of the last manufacturing companies left on Long Island, and the couple had a beautiful home, a dog, and a cat. "The one thing missing from our lives," Jon says, "was kids."

Both of them wanted children; for Rob in particular, who grew up as one of 11 children under the same roof, the idea of family meant more than two. But "we didn't know what our options were," as Jon puts it. It was the early 1980s. Few gay men had children of their own. But when a friend of theirs adopted a child, it "put the idea on the radar screen," in Jon's words, and they began actively to pursue parenthood.

Their first stop was New York's Adoption Blue Book, a listing of all the children available for public adoption statewide. One problem with taking that route was that Jon and Rob very much wanted an infant, and the Blue Book offered none. Another problem was less easy to quantify but considerably more pervasive—it would impede their attempts at private adoption as well—an only lightly disguised reluctance to place children with a gay couple. While the state "theoretically didn't discriminate," says Jon, every time he and Rob expressed interest in a child, "there was always a 'but.' " The child would be deemed "not ready," or Jon and Rob,

who are respectively white and Latino, would be told that a black family was "preferred" for a black child, or an available baby would be declared "not right" for the Cooper home. Once, Social Services deflected their interest in a 13-year-old who had been in foster care and had been abused, saying the boy needed to "stay in foster care a while longer in order for him to heal. We found out later they preferred to place him with a straight couple." Seeking-to-adopt ads placed in the newspaper elicited almost no antigay responses—thankfully—but the responses the ads did elicit led to dead ends. Their efforts were proving fruitless, and their frustration level was high.

Then they heard about a reference guide on foreign adoptions that listed each country's adoption requirements—whether a single male could adopt, what age the adoptive parent had to be, whether the adoptive parents were required to have other children, and so forth—and listed the agencies in each state that handled adoptions for the countries covered. Jon and Rob searched the book, ticking off the requirements they fulfilled, and Honduras seemed their best bet: it was willing to place children with a single male, did not require the adoptive parent to have children already, and established no age requirement.

But narrowing the choice to a single country did not make the process a breeze. The next step was to find an experienced adoption agent who could make some connection to the adoption network in Honduras. They found the right person in a small town north of New York City—she had close ties to an attorney in Honduras—and soon the private adoption of an infant boy was arranged. Jon and Rob named him Daniel.

Jon flew to Honduras to finalize the adoption. It took a couple of months, during which time he stayed at the home of his lawyer's mother, spending his days taking care of Daniel. In time for the holiday season of 1985, Jon brought home what Rob describes as "a beautiful, healthy baby boy."

Daniel's arrival prompted an important decision by the two men— the determination to be visible in the community as who they were. In Rob's words: "We were not going to isolate ourselves. Precisely because we were now raising a kid, I said to Jon that we had to be a part of the community, and we were going to be proud of our family." Both men felt strongly about this from the beginning. "As a gay Latino," says Rob, "I know how important it is to be accepted." Says Jon: "This is a socially progressive community, and we wanted to have an identity in it."

So even before Daniel entered kindergarten, Rob had become a volunteer for the special events committee, an organizer of the local Halloween parade, and "a lunch monitor at the school Daniel was about to enroll in." The aim was simple and straightforward—"so that I could build a relationship with parents and teachers," Rob says. They also became regular churchgoers at Huntington's Unitarian Universalist Fellowship, where both Jon's Jewish tradition and Rob's Roman Catholic upbringing meet and are celebrated. The growing Cooper family "went to church every Sunday," says Jon, "sent our kids to public school, and walked with them down Main Street during the annual Gay Pride celebration." They were not about to hide their light—or their family's light—under a barrel.

The growing of the family proceeded apace. When Daniel was four, the Coopers replayed their Honduran experience and adopted Jessica. Four years after her arrival, with adoption laws in Honduras suddenly more stringent, they adopted Christopher from an agency in Texas. Chris was only eight months old when the twins joined the family. Jennifer and Kimberley, like Chris, are Mexican-American, so all five children are of Latin American origin, and, thanks to their father, Rob, and language classes at school, all know Spanish—to one degree or another—as well as English.

It took 10 years in all—from 1985 to 1995—to round out the Cooper family. All the children were adopted as newborns, and all were adopted, at first, by Jon as a single parent. "We were not trying to make a political statement," Jon says by way of explanation; they just wanted their children—with as little hassle as possible. Rob was the legal guardian of the children until 2001, when in one fell swoop he adopted all five of them as a second parent.

But there's a subtle difference in the parental roles of the two men—

at least, in their children's eyes. Rob, called Papa, is the one they talk to for what Daniel calls "day-to-day life"—perhaps because he is always there—while Jon presides over the long-term issues. "Whenever any of the kids are sick, they always come to me," says Rob. "If there are problems at school and their grades slip, I say that we have to talk to Dad." Both men's families are also closely involved as grandparents, aunts, uncles, and cousins. Jon's folks live nearby, and Rob's mother and younger brother are often on the premises, although most of his siblings remain in Cuba.

Even in a big house, the older siblings can sometimes find their exu-

berant younger siblings "annoying," as Jessica has put it. But there's nothing about their family any of the children would change. Once when she was grounded and forbidden the use of the VCR, television, and computer, Jessica complained that her real mother would not have done this to her. Rob reminded her that "if she was with her real mother, she would be living in a wooden shack in Honduras with dirt floors, no electricity or running water, and there would be no VCR to turn off. She never used that argument again." To all five children, their family, in Daniel's words, is "just ordinary people living an ordinary life."

That ordinary life was very nearly shattered one day when Chris was just four years old. He had been complaining of headaches, difficulty walking, and loss of balance, but before his fathers could get him to a neurologist, they got a call from the school saying that Chris was ill and had been rushed to the hospital. An emergency CT scan and MRI revealed a brain tumor, and the doctors told Rob and Jon that "if they didn't operate immediately, Chris could die or be paralyzed," Jon says. There was no time for a second opinion. As their son was wheeled into the operating room, his fathers hugged and kissed him, uncertain "if we'd ever see him alive again." Then they held each other. Chris was in surgery for nine hours while his fathers stayed in the waiting room, bargaining with the universe. "I just kept saying to God, 'Why him? Take me instead,' " says Jon. "It was the worst day of our lives." The surgery was successful, and Chris recovered fully. Today he only vaguely remembers the operation that saved his life.

Life went on, perhaps more precious than ever. Both Jon and Rob found themselves growing more and more involved in the civic and political life of their community. Rob became a board member of Children of Lesbians and Gays Everywhere (COLAGE) and of the Empire State

Pride Agenda (New York's lesbian and gay rights organization) and served as a volunteer for a county-wide social service organization called the Family Service League. As outspoken Democrats in a heavily Republican district, the two often hosted fundraisers for Democratic candidates. But in 1997, their political involvement got much deeper. That was the year Jon was named to the Democratic Party's county committee. Shortly thereafter, he became interested in running for an open seat on the Suffolk County legislature; it was a part-time job but one that played a decisive role in local environmental policies, a passion of Jon's. So he met with his party's county executive committee, told them he was interested, and announced that he was gay. The executive committee looked at Jon's strong environmental background, and they looked at his five children, and they made him their candidate. He lost, with 38 percent of the vote, but "stayed active and ran again two years later" in 1999.

This time, it looked like he was going to win. Certainly his Republican and Conservative opponents thought so. Jon was running as a prominent businessman and active environmentalist with a record of achievement for his community; he had also visited four thousand homes in the county during his campaign. To counter his strengths, the Republicans poured lots of money into the contest, but when a poll a week before election day showed Cooper still ahead, the race turned negative. Jon's opponent raised the issue of Cooper's sexuality. Telephone canvassing and a letter-writing campaign made the case, as one letter put it, that Cooper "is a devout homosexual. He has a same-sex partner, and he's proabortion." "Do you want a homosexual representing you in the legislature?" phone bank operatives asked. As if that weren't enough, hints were dropped that Rob was an illegal alien.

Two days before election day, the powerful and prestigious Long Island newspaper *Newsday* ran a story about the campaign. The headline read: "Race Turns to Sexual Orientation"; featured in the article was the photo of the Cooper family that had appeared on Jon's campaign brochure.

Cooper was devastated. "That's it," he said to Rob. "Now all people will see is a gay guy." With virtually no time to rebut the bigotry and re-coup his lead, certain that "ten months of work had just gone down the drain," Cooper nevertheless kept up his practice of going door to door, only this time he "wanted to steal all the *Newsdays* off the driveways." He was too late, however, so he gritted his teeth and rang the first doorbell. "I admire your courage," the voter who answered the door told him. "Hang in there. This gay-bashing is disgusting." The same thing happened at the next house, and the next, and the next. It happened when a self-described "lifelong conservative" approached Rob, told him how ashamed he was, and announced his intention to vote for Jon on the Independence Party line. And it happened on election day, when Jon won the county legislator's seat with 52 percent of the vote. It was, both Jon and Rob contend, the "only time" they have ever been baited for being gay, and it backfired badly in this Republican but socially progressive part of Long Island. And lest anyone think Jon's election was simply a backlash reaction, he won again two years later with 55 percent of the vote.

In 2000, with the family healthy and Jon sworn in as county legislator, the two men held a commitment ceremony. They had "wanted to wait until we were pretty sure we wouldn't have any more kids" before holding such a ceremony, says Rob. And they were pretty sure. They had thought about it, had even been presented with an opportunity to adopt two siblings, but their older children were opposed and, says Rob, "it would have completely changed the family dynamic." The last thing he wanted was for kids who had already known abandonment and rejection to be rejected again, this time by their adoptive family. "We came to our senses and stopped where we were," Rob says.

So on an early autumn day, at the Unitarian Universalist Fellowship's castle-like home, Jon and Rob Cooper had their "wedding"—the biggest, as it turned out, ever held on the site. Seating capacity was 211, and 242 showed up, so it was Standing Room Only for the only openly gay elected county official on Long Island and his partner of nearly two decades. The happy couple's five children served as their wedding party attendants, and a *Newsday* photographer captured the event on film—an ordinary happening for Huntington, Long Island.

A Fatherhood
Not by Design

In retrospect, Steve Rosenblum will tell you that his initial understanding of what coparenting might mean was naïve at best, that his analysis of the coparenting situation he entered into was colored more by emotion than by rational thinking, and that his plan for how the "arrangement" would work was nonexistent. Despite that, and despite a coparenting experience that remains far from ideal, the result is "glorious," "wonderful," utterly "fulfilling": his daughter, Laina—called Lainey—born in 1993.

He loves being Lainey's father. "I wouldn't trade this for anything," Rosenblum says. Still, "I didn't pick the way it happened. If I were designing my fatherhood, this probably isn't the way I would have designed it."

How do you design a fatherhood? Like so many gay men, Rosenblum had assumed that his sexuality precluded the very notion of being a father. It was one of the reasons he had struggled so hard with coming out. His partner, Lonnie, had fathered a daughter in an early marriage but had little relationship with her—and regretted the estrangement. Then one day in a bar in Connecticut, Rosenblum met two gay men who each had adopted a child. "It was one of those moments," Rosenblum recalls; "I thought: 'You know, I could do this.'" Fatherhood seemed possible.

But not just yet. Lonnie was sick with HIV and in and out of hospitals. What's more, in 1990 the two men had been in a car accident that disabled Lonnie for work and left Steve as the main breadwinner and primary caregiver. There was little room for much else.

Meanwhile, Lonnie had hired a lawyer to do battle for him over the damages he had suffered from the accident. The lawyer also became a close friend. Once all the legal issues were settled, the three of them met for a celebratory dinner.

"Probably the first time I met Sue, she talked about her plans to have a child," Rosenblum recalls of the dinner. It was an abstract discussion, more theorizing than anything else, with no specifics and no follow-up. Soon afterward, Sue entered into a relationship with a woman—call her Anne—who had a young child of her own. The four "spent a lot of time together," says Steve. "Lonnie and I would babysit for Anne's daughter, and we'd all spend vacations together, so it became apparent to Sue that we liked kids a lot."

One evening in the spring of 1992, Lonnie made a lavish dinner, opened a nice bottle of wine, and said to Steve: "Now that you're sitting down, Sue and Anne want to know if you want to have a child with them."

Steve was stunned—flattered, shocked, excited, charged with "a positive burst of 'Wow!' " he recalls. It made so much sense: Here were four people who were fond of one another, got along well, and cherished children. Each had a good reason for wanting a child: Sue because her biological clock was ticking, Anne because she sought a sibling for her own child, Lonnie for several reasons, as Steve saw it. For one thing, "this represented a second chance for him, a chance to do it right" after his failure, in his eyes, with his own daughter. Moreover, "Lonnie and Sue were very close, and he felt very connected to her." And finally, Steve believes Lonnie "was taking care of me, after all my taking care of him. He was giving me something to look forward to."

With these motives, and given the closeness that tied the four together, how could they miss? "Sue and Anne had two dogs," says Rosenblum, "we had two cats, we would have two kids, and maybe one day we'd buy a two-family house." It *was* exciting. They all thought about it, talked about it, even went on vacation to think and talk more about it. Steve and Lonnie knew they wanted to "play an active, involved role as a set of dads, although exactly how that might evolve, we didn't spend much time thinking about." Instead, "we thought this would be kind of a cool, family-ish thing: the kids would split their time between our two households, and we'd do lots of family things together. At least, that was the way I thought about it." Inexorably, the thinking and talking had ripened into a decision to create a child.

Their first step was a known-donor insemination process at a local sperm bank. Steve was handed a cup and ushered into a room equipped with *Playboy* magazine. "I just laughed," he says. He proceeded to find his own way to fill the cup. "Meanwhile," he says, "I filled out a fourteen-page form on me, my family, the color of my grandparents' eyes. Then on the very last page, it asked: 'Have you ever had sex with a man?' and 'Have you ever been in a situation where you might have been exposed to a person with AIDS?' " Sue advised full disclosure, and the next day, the sperm bank destroyed Rosenblum's sperm and denied his application to be a donor. They needed to go another route.

It was just about then that Steve heard about polymerase chain reaction (PCR) testing, a direct test for the presence of AIDS that his health insurance would cover. For two months running, he came up clean, and each time, he and Sue participated in their own version of homegrown insemination. Sue became pregnant on the second try.

"The pregnancy was easy," says Rosenblum, "but the rest of our lives were in complete turmoil." Sue and Anne separated during the pregnancy, and Lonnie was declining rapidly; "he got smaller and smaller as Sue got bigger and bigger." From January 1993 forward, advancing chaos affected his lymph nodes, his skin, and finally his lungs. He died in July.

Steve had been with Lonnie for five years. But given everything else that was going on in his life, "I missed my opportunity to fall apart." He couldn't afford the time and effort falling apart would take. Sue, in an advanced state of pregnancy, was herself greatly affected by Lonnie's death. There were debts to pay and arrangements to do and undo in the wake of Lonnie's illness and dying. And a week after his death, there was a baby shower. The shift of focus from death to birth, almost surreal in its rapidity, took a toll. "I feel like I transitioned so quickly from taking care of Lonnie to taking care of a baby without ever dealing with either one," Rosenblum acknowledges years after the fact.

He was in the delivery room during Sue's very long labor, and he was in the operating room when his daughter was born via C-section. "It was amazing," he says. "After days and days of waiting, it was cut, pull, and done. Within seconds, they handed me a baby." He and Sue wanted to give their daughter a name starting with L in Lonnie's memory. Sue liked the name "Lainey," but Steve thought it sounded like a nickname, so he made up "Laina," from which it could derive. At last he was a father.

But only very part-time in the beginning. It started with Steve spending one night a week with Lainey at Sue's, not sleeping there, but "the idea was for me to be part of Lainey's home. The picture then was that Sue's was Lainey's home, and she would have a space at my home. Over time, that shifted."

One reason it shifted was that the relationship with Sue "very early on" became fraught with difficulties. "Probably within a year," says Steve, "we realized we were very different in our approach to people and in the way we communicate. We were never very different about Lainey; we have the same goals for her, share the same values, set the same limits—although we approach things differently. Our problems are with each other."

Different expectations of one another—that's what it came down to.

"I looked to Sue as the primary support person for me," Rosenblum says, "and she felt I didn't give her similar support." Their legal agreement stipulated that Sue would have the primary parenting role and Steve would have the secondary role. "I internalized my role more than she displayed hers," Steve says. "I was insecure, not very sure how this family should look—even to me. So I deferred to Sue to define my relationship with Lainey rather than defining it myself."

The strain was burdensome. It had a ripple effect. When Lainey was about three and Sue suggested the two have a second child, Steve angered her by refusing. Given the relations between them, "I didn't think it was what I wanted. I would have liked Lainey to have a sibling, but not through me."

It was hard for Steve to see his fantasy of this "cool, family-ish thing" fall apart. It soured what should have been complete joy. "Originally," he says, "I was one fourth of a plan. Then two were left. Then what we planned wasn't what I ended up with." He indicts himself for these problems, accuses himself of "naïveté and an overall lack of clarity," and he believes the original fantasy brightened what was for him a dark time. "I was at a place in my life where something exciting and wonderful could salve what was miserable." The reality turned out to be much more vexing—at times, even oppressive.

It is also irrevocable. He will always be Lainey's father, and Sue will always be her mother. To their credit, they have made substantial efforts to work through their problems, even going to counseling together to find a workable relationship they can both live with. It worked. "Sue and I got 'divorced'," says Rosenblum. "We realized we had to move away from trying to be a family to each other. Instead, we have to just be Lainey's parents and to work at that." One other result of the strain between the two is that Lainey spends more time at her father's house—three nights a week, in fact. "She needs this to be her home, too," says Steve.

The model is that of business partners. "We make mutual decisions and communicate frequently—often by email so we have time to review what we say and lower the emotional level." Steve is glad that Sue "is there to talk to"—particularly when he contemplates the arrival of puberty in his daughter—but he is also glad that he and Sue maintain their lives as two single parents. Their working rule of thumb is that "whoever Lainey is with figures it out." If she is with her father and wakes up at 3:00 A.M., "it's my problem," says Steve. "If she is sick in the morning when she stays here, I stay home from work."

Both share the financial burden, too. Lainey is covered by Steve's health insurance plan, and he pays for her after-school care and summer camp. Her clothing and living expenses are paid for by each parent in his and her separate household; they split her allowance; and both are saving for her college education.

Steve is "the homemaker Dad," as he describes himself. He sews a sash of fabric for Lainey to wear at dress-up day at camp. For pirate day, when the kids are supposed to dress in red, he cuts up one of his old turtlenecks and fashions it into a pirate blouse. He and Lainey do "craft" things together; her mother takes her to soccer practice. Lainey also excels at Nintendo, has a best friend, does well in school, and "is not shy about expressing her dislikes," according to her adoring father.

She takes in stride having two gay parents, claiming her friends don't even mention it. She has been a part of the local Gay Pride parade since she was born, until the year when it conflicted with a soccer game.

One day when she was about five, she remarked to her father: "Isn't it funny how Mommy's daddy and mommy live together?" Given the circle of adults closest to her, it must have seemed funny: both of her parents are gay and single; her grandparents on her father's side are divorced; even an aunt is single; only her maternal grandparents are married and living together.

"It is kind of funny," Steve replied.

"Are you going to marry a man?" Lainey asked him.

"I hope to."

"Mom's going to marry a woman." Lainey paused. "You know what? When I grow up, I'm going to marry a man."

It was reassurance to Steve that his daughter understood and accepted the variations possible in family life in general and her family life in particular. "She gets it," he says.

For Rosenblum, single gay parenting "can be isolating." As a single man, he finds it hard to socialize with gay couples who have kids. "I have an easier time hanging out with straight couples with kids," he says. And as a self-described "serial monogamist," he finds he is mostly "very single" as a result of focusing so much energy and attention on his daughter.

As for gay coparenting, "it can confuse people." Aware that most of his neighbors thought of him as a divorced guy with a kid, Steve felt obligated to come out to them. He does the same when people refer to Sue as his "ex-wife." But all of Lainey's teachers and all the parents at her school know the situation, and coming out is "more of a chore than anything else." There has been no lack of support.

All in all, "things are pretty good," Rosenblum says. He has tremendous respect for his coparent and is glad they have "figured out how to deal with each other." If they are not ideally suited as coparents, "we are managing it for the sake of our child—and for each other." And at the end of the day, "being a father and being with Lainey is wonderful." She calls him Dad when she's feeling grown up, Daddy when she's feeling more clingy. And after all, that's the thing he didn't want to miss out on.

The Fost-Adopt Revolution

The man of my dreams is the father of my children," says Derek Peake. "I am proud to be a man who can claim love for another man and for fatherhood. I don't want people thinking my wife is at home. The man of my dreams is at home—with our children. That goes against twenty years of stereotype that I had accepted."

It wasn't the only stereotype Peake and his partner, Ted Uno, watched crumble before their eyes as they went about building their family. There was also the money stereotype—that is, we don't have enough . . . the agency stereotype—that is, no one will want to work with us . . . and the "system" stereotype—that is, neither the law nor any court will allow us to become parents. All these long-accepted, virtually formulaic conventions evaporated easily, if not overnight, once the men decided that fost-adoption was the route they wished to follow.

Foster parenting, then adopting. "The real revolution is having children," says Ted Uno. "The most powerful way to effect the change we want in the social sphere is by becoming a family." The fost-adopt way to become a family "lets you see the transformation in the children's lives and in our lives."

It was not their original choice. Biology was. Derek Peake had "always" defined himself as a father. He had once had a relationship with a woman that had resulted in an unplanned pregnancy and a miscarriage. "It was a devastating loss that I still grieve for every day," he says, but it awakened him to both the desire and the responsibilities of fatherhood— "the support required, the things I needed to do in my life."

When he and Ted Uno met in 1994 in Oakland, California, where they still live, fatherhood was "a deal-breaker," Peake says. "I would not have partnered with anyone who did not want fatherhood. For me, it was a driving, defining thing." Ted Uno made the deal, and the two men "committed our lives together," in Uno's phrase.

Their first thought was coparenting. But exploration of the legal issues painted a frightening picture of insufficient rights for gay fathers. Moreover, when a lesbian couple they had considered coparenting with broke up, it highlighted the "issue of stability," Ted says, and prompted the men to focus on whether "this is something we really want to do."

Instead they began to look at surrogacy. Here, too, a friendship with a potential surrogate raised more questions than it answered, and with the two men starting up a nonprofit consulting company, the complications and risk struck them at the time as too much to take on.

"That was a hard period after the surrogacy failure," says Derek. "The model I had in mind wasn't turning out, and I felt my clock ticking. So if we don't coparent and we don't surrogate, what is there? I never considered adoption." Why not? He had "grown up feeling that adoption would never be allowed to us. I thought it would be expensive and long and that we would end up heartbroken." In addition, Peake admits he was focused on biological offspring. "Adopted children don't equal biological children," he remembers feeling.

So they tried something else. They joined up with a straight family that had two children and was expecting a third. "We wanted to feel the experience," says Ted Uno. Although the two families maintained separate households, they shared a house, and "all became very close very quickly," Ted recalls—"an extended nuclear family. We became godparents of their newborn and his primary caregivers till he was two and a half. It showed us how parenting styles differ and that coparenting can be difficult. It helped us define what our family would be like." And it "strengthened us as a couple," says Derek. "Seeing Ted with the kids and imagining him as the father of my children was incredibly sexy" and confirmed that they "shared intense feelings about child-rearing."

Then one day Derek and Ted got a call from friends of theirs who had been asked to foster-parent a troubled 11-year-old boy. Instead the friends had recommended Peake and Uno. "They'd be great," they told the agency; "they're helping to raise a kid now." The next day, social workers from the agency, Family Builders, came out to the house to see Derek and Ted. It was their introduction to the whole foster-adopt process, and it turned on a light bulb in their heads.

But they remained somewhat uncertain at first. "Can we do this in our lives?" they asked themselves. "Can we do this for this boy?" They began classes for foster certification and a homestudy, and in time, says Derek, "it became clear to us that we wanted to pursue it." By Thanksgiving of 1998, the pair were licensed, and visits with the 11-year-old began.

But they did not begin well. A county social worker, worried about the interaction, told the boy he would be living with a black man and a Hawaiian wife; it didn't facilitate a smooth introduction. (Derek is Filipino/black; Ted is Japanese-American.) The boy's foster family worked on his already substantial quotient of fear and distrust by asking him why he wanted to "go out there with those gay guys." After a long time in the foster system, much of it in abusive homes, fear and distrust were all this boy knew, and just before Christmas, as Derek recalls the timing, "our visits ended."

When the social worker from Family Builders brought Derek and Ted the news, she also brought an album of photos, a catalogue of other special-needs children who would love to be in a family. The two men were stunned. They had become "very invested" in the 11-year-old boy. As Derek put it to the social worker, "We're doing this because we're going to adopt this boy, not because we're going to adopt a child in the abstract." The agency representative was understanding. "I know you're going through a grieving period," she told them, "but when you do find a child and he or she does enter your home, that will make a family. This little boy may never have that."

It made for a somewhat gloomy Christmas, but by the end of March, the Family Builders social workers were urging them to proceed. "It's time," they said, and suggested that the men look again at the catalogue.

Doing so, says Ted, "brought out the worst in us. You had to confront what you're looking for: racial preference, gender, disabilities. It shows you honest truths about yourself." When they saw the file on Nicholas, age five and a half, Ted was instantly moved. "Nicholas is Thai and black," says Derek; "he looked like the two of us."

In mid-May, 1999, they and their Family Builders social worker drove to Sacramento to meet Nicholas, his foster mother, and the county social worker. Nicholas clung to his foster mother's leg at first, then allowed himself to be won over by Ted and Derek. At a second meeting, Nicholas came running out to the car to hug them. More visits followed; they were ready, Nicholas was ready, and the only problem was that the system couldn't quite catch up with the family-building that was taking place. By early June, however, Nicholas was in their home.

Both men attribute the speed of this mutual bonding to Nicholas's "phenomenal foster family." They had "addressed the two dads issue in the most loving way," Derek says, impressing on him "how great it would be." In every way possible, the boy had thrived in their care.

Originally, that foster family had been preparing Nicholas for re-unification with his mother, who suffered from depression and suicidal tendencies. She had made "extraordinary efforts," in Ted's words, "to get stable," and by the end of June, she wanted her son back.

First they tried mediation. Nicholas's mother admitted she was con-testing the termination of her rights because, as Ted remembers her say-ing, "I have to be able to tell Nicholas later in life that I did everything I could to keep him, and that it was the courts that took him away." She had no objection to Derek and Ted being gay, but she rejected the idea of an open adoption.

Five months after the mediation failed, the case went before a judge. In court it became clear to Nicholas's mother that she would not prevail. It was a matter of "best interest of the child"; Nicholas had been in dan-ger with his mother but was thriving with Derek and Ted. As she had once instigated her own son's removal from her care, she now withdrew her claim.

"It was an extraordinary moment," adds Ted. "Here's this mom who has really tried, who really loves her son. I was honoring that while fear-ing I would lose my son. I was impressed that she was willing to fight and willing to give up. It was a strange set of emotions. But what an amazing cleaver and bonder of families the law is."

Eighteen months later, Family Builders called and asked for help. There's an eight-year-old in an emergency placement who needs a home right away, the agency said. Can he stay with you until we find him a permanent home? "We're on our way over," Derek and Ted replied.

Javier had been born to a 13-year-old and had been remanded to the foster system at the age of one and a half on the grounds of medical neglect. He had been in seven different families since that time, had suffered some bad breaks—although no abuse—had a lot of psychological issues, and had been diagnosed with reactive attachment disorder (RAD), a very serious condition in which children who have failed to bond as infants grow up emotionally underdeveloped—unable to trust or love.

"It's only a temporary placement," said the agency.

"Our family doesn't work that way," Ted and Derek replied. Instead they wanted to prepare themselves emotionally to adopt Javier, and they wanted to clear it with Nicholas. The call had come on a Thursday. On Friday they talked to Nicholas. He thought it might be fun to have an older brother but hoped he wouldn't be bossy. Javier was due to arrive on Monday. The family spent the weekend helping Nicholas reconfigure his room to accommodate Javi and decorating the house. With the neighbor children, they made cutouts of their bodies and put them on the window, hung streamers, and blew up balloons.

"Javi walked in on Monday," Ted recalls, to a neighborhood welcoming party. Nicholas opened the door to him and took him by the hand, and if he was a little overwhelmed, he "certainly understood," says Derek, "that he was very much wanted." After half an hour, the neighbor kids went home, and the newly enlarged family began quietly to sort through Javi's stuff and find places for all of it. The next morning, Ted and Derek awoke to the sounds of their sons playing and laughing together. "It was so obvious that Javi belonged to our family. He doesn't look like us, but he has Ted's personality," says Derek. "He is serious and creative, whereas Nicholas is like me—an unfocused, happy-go-lucky jock."

And Javi's reactive attachment disorder never manifested itself. "We think the court-mandated diagnosis was wrong," says Derek, "and we got it reversed. It was a convenient label to explain some problems, but we haven't seen anything remotely close to it."

Both boys were formally adopted in 2001, and at the end of that year Derek and Ted got some more news they had been waiting for. "We've got a girl for you," Family Builders announced. A network of social workers in several counties had long known that the Uno-Peake family wanted a girl. The family was well liked by the network anyway—"I think we remind them why they're in the business," says Derek—so it was perhaps not entirely accidental that "we were the very first family contacted on Melany's behalf."

There was a catch. Melany's mother had been diagnosed with schizo-affective disorder, meaning that Melany was probably predisposed to the disease, although the latest evidence seems to demonstrate that the predisposition can be lowered by environment and medication. "Can we live with this?" the men asked themselves. The day after receiving the call, they had gone to see Melany's file and photo. As Ted had been struck by Nicholas's photo, so Derek was struck by Melany's. "She evoked my maternal grandmother," he says—"same cheeks, same hair curls. If I had a baby girl with a black woman, Melany could be it. It was instant recognition." They could certainly live with it.

She was just a little over three months when they first saw her—

"teeny and totally adorable," Derek says. They came home and created a nursery in the house—"it was joyous," Derek says—but once again, the system couldn't catch up with their eagerness to bring Melany home. "We pushed very, very hard," Derek says, "and no one wanted to get in the way, but the process just wasn't that fast." Nonetheless, two weeks before Christmas, their daughter was officially placed with them. Her mother sees her regularly but tells Derek and Ted they are "the dream I had for Melany." Melany's older brothers are very protective of her, and she in turn absolutely adores them.

"We're living our dream," says Derek. "God, it's a good life." They are, Ted asserts, "proud to say we're soccer moms." Derek took a course in refereeing and is a fixture in the local kids' league; he also oversees after-school programs for the district. Javi does aikido as well as soccer, and Nicholas does ballet, "which has helped him focus and control his body," his fathers say. They are "very connected" to both the Uno and Peake families, who are frequent visitors and visitees, and the household also includes two dogs, two cats, a lizard, and a 100-gallon tank full of freshwater fish. As this book goes to press, the men are thinking ahead to adopting a fourth child. They hope to provide emergency foster care for the rest of their lives.

"We're very conservative, very traditional," says Derek. They are fairly strict disciplinarians, actively involved in the parent community, well supported by friends and neighbors, and they have constructed a model of family life in which both parents are primary caregivers.

Of course, "we are constantly outing ourselves," says Derek. "Stacked up, we look like a Benetton ad. It's inescapable that we're a family. At the same time, when we're all together, people are trying to work it out. It's our greatest joy. It's idyllic: we have polite, beautiful kids, and we get to live our lives."

For the gay community, asserts Ted Uno, "family is the center of the political revolution. Family takes us from being a sterile to a vibrant community. Without children, a community simply dies out."

Unmistakably
a Family

We are a same-sex couple in Houston interested in adopting a child," the email read. "Can you work with us?" That's how Joe and Stephen Milano began the process that eventually brought their son Ruben into their lives and established, in the legal sense, the Milano family.

Neither man started with the name Milano; it's composed of letters from the original surnames of each. As partners under those separate names, Joe and Stephen had talked about adopting with almost routine regularity, but always in the abstract and always for some other time. "One of us would say it would be nice in the future," Stephen says, "and the other would agree, and nothing would come of it." Then one year, when Joe was nearing 40, "we realized it would be difficult to do if we waited much longer. We both had established careers by then"—Joe as a business writer, Stephen as an information technology manager and consultant. "We knew we wanted a child. There seemed no reason to wait."

They started by doing basic research. "We read everything we could find on-line and in print," says Joe, from books on adoption to tomes on infant care. They had ruled out having a biological child. "There seemed enough children who needed homes," Stephen says, "and we didn't feel we would be unfulfilled if we didn't create a biological child." They also closed the door on international adoption. "Whatever route we chose," Stephen says, "we did not intend to lie about our sexuality. We wanted to do this openly, and it would have been difficult to be open about being gay in the international arena."

As part of their research, they found a Houston-based lawyer with adoption experience. "Try to find an agency in Texas," she advised them; "stay local if you can." So they went on-line, checked out a number of agencies in Houston, Dallas, and San Antonio, and began sending out their emails. From a dozen sent, they received only a couple of positive responses. One small agency in Dallas replied in the negative, making it very clear that they had a policy against working with same-sex couples, "but they wished us luck anyway."

Eventually an agency in San Antonio that had never before placed a child with a same-sex couple was eager to work with them. That seemed like the best bet, so they signed up. It was July 2000, just about one year from the moment they had decided that "now" was the time to adopt. They filled out the various forms, underwent an independent homestudy, and obtained references, including a glowing one from the pastor of their predominantly gay church, the Bering Memorial United Methodist

Church, which plays a major role in their lives. They created a book about themselves and their home for the agency to show prospective birthmothers.

Then they waited.

"The months turned into many months," says Joe. While the two "knew it would take long," as Stephen says, "we really weren't entirely prepared for how long."

Fast-forward to January 2001. Joe and Stephen are starting to think about other options. Joe is back surfing the Net looking for a good deal on a book about innovative routes to adoption. He does a Yahoo search on "adoption," and it pulls up a site he's never seen before: a listing of gay-friendly adoption agencies. Joe starts hitting some links on the site. He clicks on Texas for a list of Texas agencies—gay-friendly, as he supposes—and there's the Dallas agency that had told them no but wished them luck.

It's 8:00 P.M. Joe dashes off an email to the Dallas agency along the lines of: "I see you've changed your policy about working with same-sex couples. Well, we have a homestudy and all the requirements and are ready to go. Give us a call."

By 8:30 Joe has begun to wonder if he pulled up the right link when he got the Dallas agency. He goes back to the listing of gay-friendly adoption agencies, does a search, and there are certainly none in Texas. He has made a silly mistake. He tells Stephen about it, and they share a chuckle.

At 9:00 P.M. an answer comes in from the Dallas agency. The gist of it: "Funny you should ask." No, the agency hasn't changed its policy, but they have connected with a woman who will be giving birth to a girl in June—just five months down the road—and she has specifically asked for a gay male couple, so could Joe and Stephen please fax them the homestudy.

They did so and were quickly approved by both birthmother and agency. But Joe and Stephen were not so quick to sign the agency's contract. Given the agency's policy on same-sex couples, what would happen, they wanted to know, if "we pay money and the situation falls through?" Would the agency then use the money for another situation for them—despite the fact that they were gay? Or would the Milanos be back where they started—trying to find an agency that would deal with them? In this case, moreover, Joe and Stephen were aware that they held a strong hand, if not the upper hand, in affecting the antigay policy. After all, they were doing the agency a favor—that is, serving as their only gay parents "on file" to meet the expectant mother's request.

And they had help. The agency's staff had long wanted to work with same-sex couples. The convergence of the birthmother's request for such a couple and the appearance, thanks to Joe's mistake, of Joe and Stephen gave the staff the ammunition they needed to do an intervention, as they called it, with their good-ol'-boy Texas lawyer boss. "Look," they more or less told him, "here's a stable couple with a wonderful home and great references, and here's a woman who wants her baby placed with a same-sex couple. What's your problem?" It worked. Overnight, Joe and Stephen and the office staff virtually changed the agency's policy. The Milanos' lawyer reviewed the contract, Joe and Stephen signed it, and the FedEx envelope was packed and readied for morning pickup.

That evening, February 6, an agency staff member phoned "in a tone of voice," says Joe, "that didn't sound good." The birthfather had heard that his offspring was being offered for adoption and had threatened to sue for custody. As a result, the birthmother had withdrawn the placement.

Their hopes dashed, the men felt frustrated and dejected. *But*. There was a "but," although in this case, not without complications. A baby had been born in San Antonio the day before, September 5—a boy—to a Latino mother and African-American father. Would that be a problem for Joe and Stephen? It most certainly would not.

The baby had, however, a serious medical condition. He had been born with his intestines outside the body. The condition, known as gastroschisis, occurs in one of about 10,000 to 20,000 live births. It is a congenital defect—a hole in the abdominal wall through which protrude varying amounts of intestine, which, thus exposed, become damaged from contact with amniotic fluid.

The condition is usually discovered in a prenatal ultrasound. It's then possible to ensure sterile birth conditions and quickly perform surgery that closes the hole. This baby's mother, however, had never had an ul-

trasound. She gave birth at home and was unaware of any problem till the delivery was underway, when she summoned an emergency medical technician, who whisked the baby to the hospital for the operation.

The agency gave Stephen and Joe a week to make their decision. "We knew if we saw him, we'd say yes," Stephen explains. "But we wanted to be sure we were prepared for whatever the prognosis was." Once again, they switched into high-gear research mode. They also prayed for guidance, joined by the several hundred members of their church. When they conferred with the surgeon, he told them that all of the baby's small and large intestines had been exposed and damaged and that the task at hand was simply to wait till the intestines could work. As for long-term prognosis, there was none. "He could have just a scar or he could have lifelong gastrointestinal problems," the surgeon said. "It may be years before you know."

It was Monday, February 12, 2001, when Joe and Stephen said yes. The baby, whom they would name Ruben, was a week old. He was in the neonatal intensive care unit (NICU), attended by nurses "who had never been confronted by two adoptive dads," says Stephen, but who, after the initial shock, "were great." But Ruben "had more tubes and wires in him than I'd ever seen, and to be there in that situation with all those sick children was very emotional."

Also emotional was the leave-taking by Ruben's birthmother. With several other children to care for, and without a husband or partner—Ruben's birthfather was no longer in the picture—she believed she could not manage another child. "She came into the NICU with Ruben's brother to show us what he looked like," Joe remembers. "She wondered if we would be upset if Ruben got darker. We assured her we couldn't care less about color, that we couldn't love Ruben more under any circumstances."

Both men found their son's birthmother bright and articulate. She told them she had a gay family member and knew they would be good parents and that Ruben would have "a better life" with them. They left her alone with him for a few moments. "I can't say I know what she was feeling," Stephen says, "but we will tell Ruben that his mother loved him very much."

The two new fathers left the NICU reluctantly. They went back to Houston and called the hospital daily to see if their son had eaten and digested any food. There was good news; he was doing well and was being given some sugar water. Thanks to the research they had done, Stephen and Joe knew that Ruben would probably remain hospitalized for a couple of months. "We thought we'd spend long weekends in San Antonio at first, then maybe get him transferred by ambulance to a Houston hospital," Stephen says. Only when they had him home, they reasoned, would they start their family leave from work.

They began the Friday morning commuting to San Antonio, where they spent every allowable minute in the NICU. Their constant presence became the subject of good-natured banter: the hospital personnel had rarely seen such conscientious new parents. The NICU nurses, who treated them like celebrities and referred to them as "The Guys," had to kick them out when visiting hours were over. They changed Ruben, fed him, did "everything they let us do," Stephen says. "I think they wanted to make sure we were going to act like parents. We wanted to know everything—every measurement they took, every change in Ruben's condition, everything."

Ruben started eating, and once he did, his improvement was very, very rapid. "He had excellent care and two dads who loved him from the very beginning," says Joe. And, adds Stephen, he was "a fighter" who had proved his mettle. Stephen explains: "The surgery for gastroschisis literally stuffs the organs into a chest cavity not big enough for them. That creates pressure on the lungs, so a respirator is almost always needed. But Ruben fought off the respirator. He wanted to breathe on his own."

The last Friday of the month, they arrived at the hospital in the morning as usual, met with the doctor, and got the shock of their lives. A very happy shock. "We think we'll send Ruben home Monday morning," the doctor told them. It wasn't going to be months of hospitalization after all; in fact, it was a mere 21 days.

But they had nothing in the way of baby supplies—"not even a car seat," Joe recalls. They sped to Babies R Us and quickly bought one. Their first time alone with Ruben was the three-hour drive from San Antonio to Houston; Ruben slept the whole way. Once back home, they improvised. "When we had left four days before," says Stephen, "we had no idea we'd have a baby when we got home." So Ruben had to sleep in a laundry basket the first night. Then a friend arrived with a bassinet, another brought a crib, the church threw a baby shower, and pretty soon they had everything they needed.

Joe took three months off to care for the baby full-time, and Ruben went into "really wonderful daycare" when he was four months old. He never developed any medical complications whatsoever. A second surgery tightened the closure; at the same time, a plastic surgeon made Ruben a belly button. His fathers had learned from a support group for gastroschisis that older kids are sometimes embarrassed not to have a discernible navel, so they decided to plan ahead and have the plastic surgery done. Since then, Ruben's development has been absolutely normal; his fathers would say it's been remarkable. "He said 'uh-oh' at seven months," claims Joe, and although he was "a little slow to start walking," according to Stephen, "once he started, he did it with a vengeance."

August 24, 2001, was the day the Milano family officially came into existence. Ruben was adopted, and all three members of the family took the last name Milano in honor of the fact. There is a wide-ranging extended family as well. Although Stephen's parents disapprove of their son's relationship with Joe, they love Ruben. "I expect you to treat him as a grandchild," Stephen told them, and they do, although their adamantine attitude toward gays means that Stephen and Joe keep their distance. Joe's family, an abundant tribe of aunts, uncles, and cousins in Buffalo, New York, are all thrilled about Ruben and consider Stephen an intrinsic part of the family. In addition, there are the four hundred or so fellow congregants at Bering and the entire membership list of Houston Gay and Lesbian Parents—"all versions of gay parents and biological, adopted, and surrogacy kids of all ages," says Stephen. They have great neighbors, good friends—both gay and straight—and live in a cosmopolitan city where they have never met open hostility. "Right after Rosie came out," Joe says, recalling the Rosie O'Donnell television interview, "a local news channel did a piece on us." Says Stephen: "It put a Houston face on the issue. It was a very positive story."

Ruben is well out of the laundry basket, eats everything, and has his own photo album on the family website.

Grandpa Eddie

Ed Robinson was 36 when he became the father of two teenage boys. He had taught biology in a New York City private high school for 12 years, so he was thoroughly acquainted with the whys and wherefores of adolescent kids. All kinds of kids. Tough, jaded, unstable: you name it, Robinson had seen it.

Ed Robinson had also dealt with the issues of being a black man in America, and he had dealt with the issues of being a gay man in America, and you don't survive being a gay black man in America in the twentieth century without gaining profound knowledge and some casehardened calluses on your sensibilities.

Yet Ed Robinson will tell you that he was unprepared in the extreme for the experience of being a father to two troubled boys. He had no idea of the involvement it would require, the emotional investment he would make, the toll it would exact, or the extraordinary rewards, ultimately, of having a family. "I knew nothing," he says. "I hadn't a clue."

Twenty-plus years later, Ed Robinson can reflect—without regret—that an emotional need was what propelled him into fatherhood. As a teacher, kids had always been easy for him. Once he left teaching for the business world, he missed the interaction with kids and the emotional satisfaction it provided. Then one day he saw an ad on the back of New York's classic alternative newspaper, the *Village Voice,* asking people who might be interested in being foster parents for "troubled youth" to come to a meeting at the Episcopal Mission Society. Ed went to the meeting. He listened. And when it was time to sign up for the program, he made it clear that he was gay. The fact was immaterial to the Episcopal Mission Society.

Robinson spent a year in training and evaluation to be a foster and adoptive parent, going to "a lot of meetings with others in the system—both foster parents and those preparing to be foster parents." Then he got a call from the Society; in fact, the guy on the other end of the phone was a former colleague from Ed's high school teaching days. "We have someone for you," he said; "we think this would be a good match." The guy from the Society was "very friendly," Ed says, "but he described the boy physically—very good-looking, light-skinned—as if selling him. I found it strange; it made me uncomfortable." And there was not a word about the boy's background, nothing about what it would mean to bring him home.

Sammy *was* extremely good-looking. At the age of 17, he was also "terrified," says Ed, "and I could sense it." He could neither read nor write. Abandoned by his mother when he was three, he had been cared for by a neighbor till her husband was posted to Germany; she could follow, but not with Sammy. So at the age of five, Sammy was placed into the foster care system. From then until he moved in with Ed at 17, he had lived in 10 different homes. In a number of those homes, he had been abused. When Ed wondered about the cigarette burns on Sammy's back, Sammy told him: "Don't ask."

Because Sammy was illiterate, the school assigned him to special education classes, and because this embarrassed him, Robinson arranged for a tutor. Against behavior that was almost out of control, Ed applied discipline as lovingly as he could. It was exasperating, baffling, discouraging, and very, very tough. "I was in tears from the frustration," Ed recalls. Yet there was some evidence that the discipline was working, that Ed was getting through to Sammy.

One day when he had taken Sammy back to the Society office for a scheduled evaluation appointment—a chance to raise any issues—Sammy exploded. He verbally and vociferously attacked everybody in the agency, then ran out the door, still fuming. Ed was horrified. "You're making progress," a social worker told him.

"Progress?"

"Clearly, Sammy trusts you enough to express what he really feels without fear of abandonment." The idea stunned Ed, but it was true. There *was* progress. He *was* getting through to the boy.

By the time Ed and Sammy had been a family for six months, it was evident that Sammy was softening. He felt free to invite friends over. He joked that he was turning into a social worker's success story. And he called Ed "Daddy."

Just after that Christmas of 1980, the Society called and asked Ed if he could take 16-year-old David on an emergency basis, "just for a month or so till another foster home opens up." Ed agreed.

David's arrival immediately sparked a jealous rivalry between the two boys, as they fought for Ed's attention. If Sammy's troubles were written on his face and told in his behavior, David's intelligent and outgoing demeanor made him seem untroubled. But he was as damaged as Sammy, Ed says; "he just hid it better." David's biological father, according to the agency, was an institutionalized alcoholic, while his mother exhibited such erratic behavior—possibly due to a brain tumor discovered later—that David had been removed from her care. Hence the "emergency" placement. But when the "other" foster home did not "open up," Ed told the Society to "leave him with us."

It wasn't easy. While David *seemed* to be settling in well, preparing to enter Brooklyn College in the fall, Sammy was going through a horrendous adjustment, and he was putting Ed through hell. "He was supposed to go to the tutor, but he didn't. He just hung out. I made constant attempts to get him into a setting, some sort of setting"—some structured environment in which a routine could be established. "Nothing worked."

Time was running out. At 18, the foster care system, in Ed's phrase, "dumps you. They give you a course in independent living and a stipend, and they're finished with you. You're officially out of the system." Sammy stayed with Ed. He blew most of his stipend on clothes. The rest of it in no way covered Ed's expenses. "He went through a gallon of OJ a day," Ed says, not to mention solid food, clothing, and the myriad other costs a grown young man incurs. Now there was even more time to hang out. And Sammy's behavior grew even more unbalanced. Ed was certain "he was using drugs and alcohol." That's not good for anyone, but it's particularly bad for a severe asthmatic, which Sammy was.

He was also officially out of the system, and the Society wanted him out of Ed's house. "You're stunting Sammy's independence," the social workers told him, and they urged Ed to "push him out." Sammy stayed. But he was becoming unmanageable. As he often had, Ed offered to adopt Sammy, and as he always did, Sammy refused. "My presumption," says Ed, "is that he thought he wasn't worthy." Sammy routinely compared himself unfavorably to David—now living in a dormitory on the Brooklyn College campus—as if David were worthy of adoption but not he. "Besides," he told Ed, "you'll always be my father, so it doesn't matter." But the crazed behavior continued. Sammy was on the premises—although less and less—but there seemed to be no one home. He heard, but he didn't listen. There was just no response to Ed's love, worry, concern; no way to stop the downward slide into drugs, bad company, the streets.

"I'll find you a place," Ed finally told him. "There's nothing more I can do." He got him a single-room occupancy unit at the Brooklyn Y, but it's likely that Sammy lived mostly on the streets. All Ed knows for sure is that when Sammy moved out, he took with him all the photos of himself that Ed had taken. Ed can't understand "the psychology of why he felt he had to remove all that."

In 1984, Sammy was arrested in a sweep of drug dealers and users. Ed was able to intervene and have him placed in a long-term care program in which he could both treat his addiction and get an education. "He tried it for a while, but he couldn't do it," Ed says plaintively. Sammy went back to the streets. Sometimes he would phone Ed: "Come have a meal with me," he'd say. And sometimes he'd come and stay with Ed in his new house in New Jersey, where he had moved in 1985—although the suburbs, Sammy told Ed, "are not for me." The last time Ed saw him was at the house in New Jersey. "He took my VCR," Ed says.

One of Sammy's street friends came and told Ed that Sammy had died. He had been doing cocaine. For an asthmatic, doing cocaine is like playing Russian roulette. Sammy lost. He was 22. His body was cremated, and his ashes, says Robinson, "will go with me."

When Ed Robinson speaks of his son, Sammy, one gets the impression of a wayward but blazing light that burned itself out in its brief course against the sky. It didn't have to be that way. The damage was imposed from outside; it was Sammy who paid the price.

How do you cope with such a loss? David seemed "indifferent," and Ed "didn't have a clue of how I was feeling." He was simply stunned, uncomprehending, uncertain what he was supposed to feel. After a few weeks, he went to a gay retreat house run by a lay order of the Episcopal Church. "That's where the grief hit me like a ton of bricks," he says.

He began to drink. "I was always a drinker," Ed says, "but after Sammy's death, I became A Drinker." A year later, Ed entered a recovery program. It took a lot of AA meetings and a lot of therapy for him to accept that he had never had the power to rescue Sammy—no one did—and on the tenth anniversary of Sammy's death, "I finally stopped blaming myself for it."

Meanwhile, David continued to hide his own psychological and emotional damage, even as he added to it a sense of neglect as Ed focused on keeping Sammy alive, then on dealing with his death. David had been "extended" in the foster care system past the age of 18 because he was a college student, but when he dropped out, that was it. He came home to Ed and duly found a job. But "nothing was going well for him," Ed says.

"He was floundering." Ed advised him to go into the service. "I thought he needed structure, discipline," he says.

So in his early twenties, David entered the Air Force, where he found structure, discipline, and a chance to learn certain important skills. When he came out of the Air Force, he added to those skills by going to computer school. And once he graduated, he began a career as a local area network administrator, working for a hospital, a transit agency, and a range of corporations. He also married and divorced three times in his twenties and thirties, fathering two sons along the way. Now David seems to be in a stable and mature relationship with a woman, and his sons are responsible and appealing young men—and the apple of their grandfather's eye.

Yet Ed believes that his son, David, like Ed himself, is still searching, looking to repair the loss that any child suffers when a parent is lost to him at an early age. Today, Ed and David have a very good relationship— "We've both grown a lot," Ed says—and he is particularly proud of the strong relationship David maintains with his own sons. It is evidence to him of how far David has come in his process of growth.

With his grandsons, David Junior and Alynn, who is pictured with him, Ed is admittedly "indulgent." He has been able to experience with them the little-kid things he never had with his own sons: Christmas shopping, the circus, visits to the amusement park. He has also taken them to Gay Pride marches, and when one of them, as a little boy, showed an interest in dolls, Ed was supportive. He is close to the boys, and he is close now to their father, and he is "starting to notice how much love there is in this world."

Once, being black and gay had given him a "feeling that the world was out to get me. There was a generalized 'them' out there, and I de-

veloped a paranoia about hiding who I was, trying to convince this
'them'—and me—that I was somebody else."

His own family disapproved of his sexuality and at first was not
friendly to Sammy and David, although they later grieved with Ed when
Sammy died, and they love the grandchildren. And real partnership with
another man has always eluded Robinson. Instead, there has been a series of relationships—none of them lasting. "But being a father and a
grandfather and growing older changes things," Robinson says.

"There are two levels of being out," he goes on. "To the world, and
to yourself. I was out to the world in my twenties, going to gay-identified
places and having gay-identified friends. I thought I was out when I be-

came a foster parent. But now I'm out at another level: living a life that I enjoy without looking for The Life—that whole collection of expectations—what to wear, how to act, heavy drinking, anonymous sex, the things I was supposedly supposed to do as a gay man. It was like looking for a role model in all the wrong places. I'm finished with that."

And the life he is living seems to him "extraordinary," Ed Robinson says. "I never know what's going to happen or who's going to turn up." He is finding that "being gay seems not to be an issue anymore. Maybe kids haven't been taught to hate so much." He wants young gay men who may be ambivalent about the impulse to be a parent to know they can do it. It's one reason Robinson belongs to a gay fathers organization, a group of men who became fathers during their marriages, then left their marriages and came out. Ed is the first foster or adoptive parent in the group, but to him, it's the name that counts—Gay Fathers—so that gay men thinking about fatherhood will know it can be done. "The world says you shouldn't or you can't? Do it," says Ed Robinson.

Because it's worth it. "It will change your life completely, and certain friends won't like the fact that you've done it, and you may face ostracism from certain gay people, but the reward is unbelievable. You grow up. You begin to see life as a whole different process. You learn what love is at a level where you haven't given or done much of anything to deserve it, but you receive it anyway."

His son calls Ed Robinson Dad, and his grandsons call him Grandpa Eddie. The only other person ever to call him Eddie is his mother.

Patience

O ne step at a time." That's what Ted Scheffler told himself somewhere along the zigzagging route to the adoption of his child. "If this is meant to be, each step will go okay." It was an attitude that would allow him to maintain both balance and hope through a series of seesawing vicissitudes.

Scheffler had always wanted to be a parent. He got confirmation that it was something he could do when he first came east from California to teach in a Harlem middle school in New York City. There he learned that he could make a difference in the lives of the "rough and unhappy kids" who made up the majority of his students, 90 percent of them in foster care and, in Scheffler's words, "not living a very good life." To this upper-middle-class white man, Harlem was "a whole new world," one in which his skin color sometimes made him an object of suspicion, even hostility. But he found it was "the work you do with the kids" that counts. "I grew to love them, and they grew to love me." He wanted to adopt a child in Harlem, but this was a time when New York City adoption agencies were extremely wary of placing an African-American child with a white parent, particularly a single, gay, white parent.

Scheffler decided to try another route. Some acquaintances were part of a group planning to adopt in China; they told him one family had dropped out. Would Ted be interested? He thought hard about it. He hadn't at first seen himself as the parent of a Chinese child, but when he thought of the need for adoptive parents—of Chinese girls being abandoned by their parents—he decided he would do it. In August 1995 he filled out an application.

His partner at the time was also interested in adopting. In fact, the shared desire to have a family had been one of the things that brought the two together in the first place. They were living in Brooklyn at the time, where Ted was then teaching, and as they began to search for a bigger apartment and alerted their families, Ted grew more and more excited. So it was a blow when his partner began to back off. By February 1996, the partner had changed his mind about the adoption altogether. It sundered their relationship and was the direct cause of their breakup.

How can I do this alone? Ted now wondered. *Can* I do this alone? He thought about single mothers and figured that they managed somehow. I'll treat it like that, he decided, and continued to take it one step at a time.

When the orphanage director—call him Mr. Wong—came to the

United States, he met with Ted and promised to find him a child. They began corresponding, yet time after time, when the orphanage found a child for Ted, Chinese officials shot it down.

First, he was offered a five-year-old girl, but because Chinese law requires an adoptive parent to be 40 years older than a child of the opposite sex, and because Ted was then 38, that adoption fell through.

Then Mr. Wong found two boys for Ted, a five-month-old and a five-year-old. Figuring that the five-month-old had a better chance of being adopted by a family, Ted said he would take the five-year-old. When the five-year-old was found to have a heart condition—in China, the physical exam takes place *after* the agreement to adopt—Chinese

medical officials said he could not leave the country. As a "consolation," Ted was offered a three-year-old girl. Once again, he agreed, and once again, his hopes were disappointed.

Then one night, he was reading the Gospel according to Matthew in his copy of the New Testament. There were "two reasons," Scheffler says. One reason was Ted's born-again Christian brother, who claimed the Bible as a basis for his disapproval of Ted's sexuality. Ted figured that if he were to defend himself, he had better go to the source to know what the argument against him was. Another reason was to find out what this particular gospel had to say about patience. "It says that God has a plan," Scheffler asserts, "and that seemed appropriate to what I was going through."

The next day, he learned that a Chinese court had determined that the five-month-old boy Ted had thought would go to a family should go to "Mr. Scheffler" after all. It was June 1996; Ted had been on the adoption roller-coaster since the previous September. Patience, indeed. He decided to name his son Matthew. Only later did he learn that it means "gift of God."

He flew to China on June 30. "Matthew was in my arms July 2," he recalls, but the boy was a very sick five-month-old. "For the first couple of days, he was really out of sorts," says Scheffler. "He didn't cry for a bottle, and he wasn't very responsive at all. But then his fever broke, and as I was giving him a bottle, he looked up at me and smiled." Scheffler pauses. "It gave me chills," he says. He felt the connection as an instantaneous and palpable bonding, a meeting of soulmates. This is how new mothers feel, he thought. Women he knew had told him that they could hear their unborn fetus crying inside when they were pregnant, and Ted had always assumed that such a feeling was denied to him as a man—especially as a gay man. But the link he felt to his child at that moment—and every time he heard him cry throughout his infancy—seemed to him incredible, intrinsic, unbreakable. He silently vowed to Matthew that he would stop at nothing to help him be the best that he could be.

Back home in the States, life quickly settled into a routine. Ted would give Matt his first bottle in the morning, then a nanny would take over till Ted arrived home from teaching school at 3:00 P.M. "He was a very easy baby," Ted recalls, "as if God knew I needed that."

Still, there wasn't room for much more in life. It was virtually impossible to date a man who had no interest in children. Some men he dated thought they wanted to be parents—then got cold feet when they saw what it was like. Or they resented Ted's commitment to Matthew and were jealous of the time, energy, and affection Ted bestowed on his son. Others thought they knew how to parent better than Ted and tried to take over. He remembers one man who berated Ted for the way he put Matthew to sleep at night. Another upbraided him for being "too fussy" about wiping Matt's runny nose. Yet another was frustrated that Ted didn't hire more babysitters so they could go out more. Ted began to despair that he would never meet someone "who would let me be the father I wanted to be to Matt, not try to take over, and want to be in a relationship with me, not just with my son."

He met Bernard Figueroa in 1999, when Matthew was three and a half. Bernard was interested in adopting and eager to talk to someone who had done it, so mutual friends suggested he phone Ted. For his part, Ted was and is "always willing to talk to gay men who want to adopt," so the two arranged a meeting at a bookstore for the next day.

Ted was two hours late—"That hasn't changed," Bernard remarks dryly—and Bernard "actually waited for us," Matt recalls, something else

that hasn't changed. They caught up with one another in the bookstore's children's section. It was nearly time for Matthew to be put to bed, so when Ted invited Bernard home for a chat, it was on the understanding that "you'll have to wait till I put him to bed."

Bernard remembers watching father and son brush their teeth, then disappear into the nightly ritual of bedtime. He liked what he saw. The two men stayed up till two in the morning talking about relationships in general, the difficulties of dating as a parent, life and how to live it.

The relationship between the California-born schoolteacher and the French designer of women's shoes flourished, as the two—the three— found much in common. At the time, Bernard owned a cabin in the mountains north of New York. Ted and Matt came for a visit, and all three went tramping through the woods. They had a wonderful time together. When Ted and Matt flew out to Seattle for a vacation, Bernard joined them. They explored offshore islands in Puget Sound, wallowed in hot springs, stayed in small hotels and at campsites. "Traveling like that shows who you are," Ted asserts; "it showed us we were meant for each other." When they got home to Brooklyn, Bernard moved in.

"At first, I was like a guest, and it was really nice—wonderful—just to look at Ted and Matt," says Bernard. "It was kind of a movie." In time, he goes on, he became a player in the movie, and the three of them grew into a family. Ted equates the process to weaving, with Bernard interlacing himself into the tightly stitched duo till he became "a part of it all," and Matthew could proclaim: "I like that there's three of us."

But it didn't happen overnight, and it wasn't entirely pain-free. Matthew at first had trouble sharing Ted with Bernard; he resented the closeness that was evident between the two of them. Bernard, deeply conscious of the life Ted and Matthew had together, sensitive to its specialness, and unwilling to interfere with it, practiced patience. As for Ted, he had thought it would be "so wonderful to have a partner to share with," and it was. But he had not counted on having to let go of his exclusive role as Matt's father. "As Bernard became more of a family member and Matt grew closer to him, I started feeling jealous. When Matt went to Bernard for certain things, I felt a pang." He pauses. "I knew I had to overcome that," he goes on, "but it's a normal thing, I think."

It was all normal, but it wasn't without its stings.

Is there a relationship without stings? Ted and Bernard work at taking the bane out of theirs. They say they often look to straight couples to see how they manage such issues as jealousy between parents. These couples serve as "positive examples" for them. They believe there are reasons for the difficulties they encounter, and "if we have an argument," according to Bernard, "we do a checkup afterwards and analyze and evaluate it. It's very positive."

And they try to keep in mind some basics. "I don't want to take away from the relationship Matt and Ted have," Bernard says. "I don't want to change it. When they two are together, I love to see it." At the same time, Ted loves "seeing the relationship grow between Bernard and Matt. It makes me happy because I see it's giving Matt what he needs." He remembers his vow to help Matt be the best that he can be; he believes Bernard can help that happen.

Matthew is well on his way. The family now lives in Asbury Park, New Jersey, in an old colonial house on a tree-lined street just four blocks from the ocean, and Matt goes to school in the nearby town of Long Branch, where Ted teaches. He's into Power Rangers, likes gymnastics, is learning to play the piano, and loves to read. He notices differences, Ted says, like the fact that one father, Ted, is blond and blue-eyed, while the other, Bernard, is dark. And his fathers point out differences in others, teaching their son that there is a world of differences, all interesting, their existence enriching.

When Matt went into first grade, an after-school aide began referring to him as "Jackie Chan." Naturally, the kids latched onto it, and Matt eventually perceived the name as a pejorative. So Ted and Bernard rented a bunch of Jackie Chan movies and watched them with Matt so he could see how cool it was to be called "Jackie Chan," how it meant Matt was strong, sharp, agile, a winner.

Ted also asked for a conference with the aide. She had meant "Jackie Chan" as a compliment, she said. Yes, Ted said, but consider the consequences. "I love Aunt Jemima syrup on my pancakes," he told the African-American woman, "but I wouldn't call you Aunt Jemima." Point taken.

When Ted adopted Matt in China, he did so as an openly gay man. The director of the orphanage knew Ted's sexual identity but decided "we just won't mention it." So while Ted didn't compromise his integrity, the orphanage director may have been willing to do it for him. But *would* Ted compromise his integrity? Would he closet himself to get a child, a sibling for Matt? Given the goal, yes, he would.

It's not an issue. China has pretty much closed adoptions to singles, and when Ted and Bernard think about adopting a sibling for Matt—and they do—they think about an older child and about serving as foster parents first. "It would be nice to have a family with Bernard," Ted says.

Matthew calls Ted Daddy and Bernard Papa. "As long as he treats me like a parent," says Bernard, "I don't care what he calls me."

Daddy's Embrace

Our society perceives African-American males as disposable," says Don Hammonds, himself an African-American male. "Black boys are not considered desirable candidates for adoption. It is racism at its worst. That is why our priority has been to adopt African-American boys." So far, Hammonds and his partner, Joe Chekanowsky, who is white, have adopted two African-American boys, and they plan to adopt more.

Hammonds had always wanted to be a parent. By his early twenties, he was pretty sure he was gay, so he "didn't think it would work." Still, he remained "very closeted"—partly, he says, because of the "dislike of gays by the African-American community." A newspaperman, Hammonds moved from St. Louis to Pittsburgh in 1984 to write for the *Pittsburgh Post-Gazette,* and there he met Joe Chekanowsky—Joey—and fell in love for the first time. "It was a shock," he says. Two weeks later, the men decided to live together. They shared important values, Chekanowsky asserts; among them was the desire to have children.

But for nearly 10 years, according to Hammonds, they went "back and forth on the whole issue." Then in 1993, they were vacationing in Provincetown, Massachusetts, and came upon a book called the *Handbook of Gay Parenting.* "The book seemed something of an omen," Hammonds says. "We decided at that instant that it was time."

So Hammonds gathered up his courage and made a call to Black Adoption Services, arranging for a meeting with a caseworker the next day. He was concerned about antigay discrimination and said as much to the caseworker. "We can't discriminate," she told him. The city of Pittsburgh had passed a gay rights ordinance, and discrimination was against the law. "So let's proceed," she suggested.

"The next thing we knew," says Joey, "she was arranging to do a homestudy and giving us individual tests." When the results came in, the caseworker "looked stunned," Don Hammonds says. "This is a first," she told them. "You have exactly identical answers. Clearly, you're better prepared to be parents than most straight couples. You will get a baby."

The two were overjoyed, but their happiness was short-lived. A three-year-old boy in county custody was referred to them, but when the county agency found out the two were gay, agency staff refused to place him in their home. Don and Joey were devastated. They had reconfigured their lives, going so far as to buy furniture for a child's room. "Joey didn't talk for days," Don recalls.

Their caseworker said she would try a private agency next, but Don was certain any private agency would be particularly conservative, and "I gave up all hope." Of course, the agency had to be informed that Don and Joe were gay. "Oh, good," they said when they heard—"our first gay placement." Don was flummoxed: a public agency had discriminated where a private one had not. It didn't jibe with his preconceived assumptions.

He didn't have much time to remain perplexed. That very afternoon, Hammonds and Chekanowsky were asked if they would adopt a four-month-old baby boy who was living in a foster home. "Write a letter to the birthmother," the caseworker suggested to Don. All he knew about the mother was that she had several other children and simply could not afford to raise another, but she still had the option to choose who her child's adoptive parents would be. She had been shown the Hammonds-Chekanowsky homestudy, so Don wrote about his hopes and dreams for the baby she had given birth to. She wept on reading it; later she told them they were the parents she wanted for her child.

That night, Joey and Don headed for the mall to shop for baby clothes, diapers, cribs, bassinets, and all the other essential baby paraphernalia. "Who's having the baby?" the saleswoman in the baby department asked them. "We are," they answered in unison. She laughed. "How wonderful," she said; "let me give you some tips." "That was the reaction we got everywhere," Joe says. The next week, they went to the foster home to pick up their son, Brenton. "They put him in my lap," Joe recalls, "he pooped, and I burst out crying." It was June 1994.

They knew that Brent had been born prematurely, and they had been given what was billed as "a thorough study" of his background. But that study "didn't cover all the bases," Don says. They would learn that he had toeing-in, so that getting around could sometimes be painful, and he also developed sensory integration dysfunction, an inability to process certain information received through the senses, which occupational therapy and other services are expected to modify. But none of this dampened by an iota Don's and Joe's joy in their son, who was overall "pretty healthy, even rambunctious." And because he had been much loved by his foster family—his foster mother made him a quilt and sent Don and Joe a letter about his likes and dislikes—attachment was never a problem.

The new family became official as soon as it was possible—which took a little over two years. With state law murky on the issue, it was decided that each father would adopt as a single parent in turn. Don thus became, according to the social worker, the first openly gay man in the

county to adopt a child. He feared the process would be difficult—if only because it was novel—but in fact it was a "mostly positive" experience. Joey adopted Brenton a year later.

When Brent was about a year old, Joey and Don founded Families Like Ours. It's a combination support group, babysitting co-op, and community organization. It's made up of some 70 families, both gay-and-lesbian families and straight families "who value diversity," Don says. They all get together every third Sunday for "potluck, play, emotional support, and feedback." The group has become an extended family for all the adults and children in it, and it remains a mainstay of the Hammonds-Chekanowsky household.

When Brent was three, Joe and Don decided to adopt a second child. They again applied through Black Adoption Services. This time the child in question was already 14 months old. He had been in the care of a foster mother who was herself plagued by so many personal health problems that she had virtually turned over the care of the baby, Jorian, to her 11-year-old daughter. All the foster mother did, Don reports, was to hold Jorian, which was what the medical experts recommended as a way to counter the drug withdrawal he went through as an infant. "He lived on her breast and shoulder," Don says. "He had never gone outdoors, never been to a playground," received little stimulation, had been introduced to neither toys nor books, and could barely babble.

Bringing him home made for a difficult adjustment. For one thing, Brent felt betrayed and took it out in anger directed at Joey. Jorian, in his turn, could not comfort himself for the loss of his foster mother; this was manifested in his inability to sleep at night. "Night after night, we would sit at his bedside as he cried," Joe recalls. "We didn't know how to get him to sleep. He would reach out to be picked up, then suddenly stiffen with grief. It was very difficult." They learned that "adopting an older child is dramatically different from adopting an infant," says Don.

They also learned one of the most important lessons of adopting, says Joey—that you have to ask for help. There are things you have to have, he maintains, and no one person or organization can provide them all, so you need to ask for help, advocate for it, agitate for it if necessary. What things? At a minimum, says Joey, "you may have to have intervention, in-home therapy, counseling services, social services, a supportive network of friends and family."

They certainly had the latter. In addition to Families Like Ours, they had the unqualified support of their church, the good will of neighbors, and the love and practical support of Don's family—though not of Joe's family, from which he is estranged. Families Like Ours alone provides their children "a huge network of uncles and aunts and cousins," not a single one of whom is related by blood. The children also have a loving grandfather who is thrilled to have one grandson, Brenton, who is a natural athlete, and another, Jorian, who is creative and very adept at building things. The boys have two loving aunts, Don's sisters, who adore them. When strangers wonder about them—an interracial couple, two dads—the reaction is almost always positive: A family? Wow! We didn't even know you could do that! How great!

But of course, not every reaction is positive, and support and goodwill are not universal.

"Joey called me at work one day," Don Hammonds recalls, "to tell me what had happened in the store. An African-American woman in Afro garb, a Christian fundamentalist, was offended that a white man had Jorian and demanded to know how he got the child. Joey thought she was aggressive and knew she was asking things that were none of her business, so he tried to ignore her. She said, 'What does your wife think of you having a black baby?' and Joey said, 'I have a partner.' So she grabbed hold of Jorian and started screaming that his father was the devil and he shouldn't stay with him."

Joey takes it from there. "I was yelling at her to get her hands off my child, and no one was coming to my aid. Everyone just watched. It was a tug of war. Then a friend interposed herself between us and broke her grip. Jorian ran and hid, and we eventually got out of there." They also eventually took the woman to court.

There were times when it seemed they could not go out as a family without "*someone* commenting," as Don puts it. After all, their sons look different from one another and very different from one of their fathers. Jorian is copper-complexioned and green-eyed, and people are constantly asking "what he is." "African-American," Don routinely answers. Once, in a museum, "an upper-middle-class white mother" shooed her children away from the Hammonds-Chekanowsky family as if their proximity might be contaminating. Because Don and Joe don't want their children to grow up ignorant of racism, they explained to them that not everyone will always like them—some people because they have two dads, others because of their skin color—but that many, many people love them very much and always will.

What Don describes as "discrimination both racial and sexual from both black and white" is painful all around, yet what perhaps hurts Don the most is his sense that "African Americans have way more problems with the idea of gays being parents and with the idea of gay men being parents of African-American children." More than once he has found himself in a "scuffle" with other African Americans about "how I rear my children." A woman at a fair one day commented that Brent was well-mannered, quiet, and polite, then wondered: "But how can he function without street sense?" Don was ready with an answer. "He'll function fine," he said, "because he won't be in the streets. I don't believe in street sense," he went on. "I believe kids need to be protected until such time as they are ready to take care of themselves." The woman turned away in a huff. It was a tough moment for a man who sees himself as "trying to give pride in African-American ethnicity without arrogance."

Don and Joe are "strongly determined to rear our children to be welcoming, healthy, sensitive, and expressive young men," Don says, "free from emotional repression, arrogance, or disrespect." They want their sons to know they "don't have to follow the boy code," adds Joey—the stereotyped gender role differentiations—"just their own code, what their heart tells them."

But with all the variants of discrimination that their boys may face in their lives, the two fathers are aware that the core issue is the fear with which so much of our society regards black men. As a result, black boys are shunned, Don says, "on the theory that they will grow up to rape and break heads." It is a kind of systemic racial profiling, although the fear, like all fears, is irrational, and "nothing," as Don asserts, "could be further from the truth" than the idea that these boys will grow up to be bad or scary men.

Of course, he goes on, "if children don't get certain kinds of nurturing and development as infants and toddlers, you can pretty much hang it up, but we refuse to listen to that truth in this country, so we have thousands of African-American boys with no homes." He claims that most of the African-Americans incarcerated in the nation's prisons "are the products of the foster care system. They have no idea of family, no sense of other people's feelings, little concern for others. That's why they're in that situation."

Against this, Don and Joe have felt the need to support, nurture, and care for black children as their sons. "I want my kids to know that no matter what they do or where they go, Daddy's arms are here to embrace them," says Don.

But not just his kids. Don is studying to be a minister with a strong counseling background; he hopes to use his ministry and his numerous other community affiliations as a forum for children's issues. Joey is the full-time dad. He finds it both "stressful" and "a great time." He was an accountant before he was a stay-at-home parent, and he hopes one day to get back to that, but for the moment he finds his role as a father fulfilling.

Don and Joe give each other one night out a week, but their children are their full-time commitment. "Just having those kids there to nurture," says Joey, "to watch them grow, to see the looks on their faces: that's the best part." He pauses. "And the hugs," he adds.

Love,
Equal and Shared

Will Halm and Marcellin Simard had so much trouble finding a reliable surrogacy agency willing to work with same-sex couples that Will eventually formed his own. He and Gail Taylor, a veteran professional in the surrogacy field and herself the mother of an alternatively inseminated child, together created Growing Generations in Los Angeles, the second largest surrogacy agency in the world and the first to place primary focus on helping gay individuals and couples. All three Simard-Halm children were born through surrogacy, the last in 2002 with a Growing Generations surrogate—while the next child, a fourth Simard-Halm, is "in planning" as of this writing.

Will, a lawyer, and Marcellin, a cardiologist, became life partners in

1986 and began to explore parenthood in 1990. There seemed "lots of obstacles to adoption," says Will. Agencies were "not encouraging" about
domestic adoption, and the men themselves were wary of foreign adoption. They worried about countries like China, where the doors to single
men were closing; as for those countries in which gay adoptions were
frowned upon, Simard and Halm were not comfortable with the idea of
closeting themselves to obtain a child. So, "out of necessity," says Simard,
they began putting out the word to family and friends that they were
looking for a woman willing to carry and deliver a child for them. At the
time, says Halm, "we didn't even call it surrogacy." It was just a way to
become fathers that would give them some control over the process—or
so they hoped.

They "hooked up with three different and not altogether appropriate women," Halm relates, "none of whom got pregnant—thank good-
ness." But it was a time-consuming and disheartening process. They went
to "a couple" of surrogate agencies, Will recalls, but were repeatedly told
"we'd be a long shot because we're gay. 'Find your own surrogate,' they
told us." So they did.

A colleague of Marcellin, who had also been a close friend for several
years, "saw how much we wanted kids and offered to carry a child for us.
She had a child already, and she just wanted to do this for us. And her
husband agreed. But she didn't want to be biologically related."

The two men had another friend, a "recent college graduate," as Will
describes her, who "knew we wanted kids." So Will "took her out to
lunch one day, and after salad, I popped the question: 'Would you consider being an egg donor?' " She said she would, so Simard and Halm
now had two of the key players in what is called gestational surrogacy (as

opposed to traditional surrogacy, in which the surrogate's own eggs are inseminated with semen from a prospective father). Will, still working in the corporate environment at the time, drew up the contracts among the parties, and they were ready to try to make a baby.

Another colleague of Marcellin, a physician skilled in in vitro fertilization, coordinated the medical process, although Marcellin actually administered the medication necessary to synchronize the reproductive cycles of the egg donor and surrogate. Other separate therapies were aimed at stimulating various pregnancy-inducing processes. Eggs were then extracted from the egg donor, and Halm and Simard supplied the sperm. Four embryos were created and frozen for storage.

The first insemination attempt did not work; the second resulted in a pregnancy, but the surrogate miscarried. Two frozen embryos were left. Since the typical procedure is to "use the best first," as Will says, their doctor gave them only a 20 to 30 percent chance for conception from the remaining embryos. "This was our low point," Will recalls. "We had spent a fortune, we had gone through a lot, and our chances did not look good." The men decided that if this next attempt didn't work, "we'll give up."

Instead, "miraculously," as Marcellin says, one of the two remaining embryos "took." Their healthy surrogate went through a healthy pregnancy, and Halm and Simard were on hand at the hospital when their daughter, Malina, was born.

That was 1996. They knew they wanted another child through surrogacy, and almost immediately after Malina's birth, they began to search again for a surrogacy agency that would help a gay couple. They had heard of one agency in Orange County—a one-woman business—reputedly willing to work with same-sex couples. So they signed up—as

did a number of gay couples—paid the fee, and watched as the one-woman business went bankrupt and the woman and their cash disappeared across the state line.

Yet two positive consequences resulted from that debacle. First, through the good graces of an assistant at the now defunct agency, they had been put in touch with a wonderful surrogate, although it was clear that they would again have to manage the process themselves.

Second, says Will, "we hooked up with other disappointed couples to talk about suing the woman, to stop her from preying on other gay couples." No one really had the stomach for litigation, but the situation stimulated an idea in Will's mind. "Knowing so much on the legal side and having been through it myself," says Will, "I thought I could start something for other gay men."

Meanwhile, Halm and Simard found an egg donor agency that would work with them. It meant that this time the egg donor was anonymous. The in vitro process yielded six embryos, one of which became their son, Luc, born in 1998 after another relatively easy pregnancy for the surrogate.

The two men decided two children were enough. They reasoned it would be "easier to afford college and other things" if they limited the size of their family, and they prepared to retire the pacifiers for good. Will, meanwhile, was talking to lots of people within the L.A. gay community about the surrogacy option, so it perhaps was not surprising that one day at the Gay Pride Festival, he and Gail Taylor should cross paths.

Their paths had actually crossed once before, back when Taylor had been working at one of the surrogate agencies that had turned down Halm and Simard because they were gay. Taylor, a lesbian, had gone on to found Growing Generations, a traditional surrogacy agency helping women receive artificial insemination of their own eggs. "We talked," Will says simply, "and it was a natural that we should join forces and form an all-around professional surrogacy agency for the gay community."

In 1998, that is exactly what they did. Will gave up corporate law to devote himself full-time to Growing Generations. What made his role particularly important was that he had been responsible for obtaining a noteworthy court judgment granting dual paternity—with both men named as fathers from birth and no maternity noted—during the surrogate's pregnancy. With that precedent serving as the "calling card" of Growing Generations, the agency is pretty much able to ensure that its clients' names are on the birth certificate. Will hopes to continue to break legal ground for gay fathers. "As a domestic partner who is infertile," he says, hinting at the next arena of advocacy, "I hope to see insurance companies pick up some of the costs of surrogacy in the future."

The costs are not inconsiderable, but then neither is the surrogacy process. Growing Generations staff estimate that a traditional surrogacy can range in price from $40,000 to $65,000, and that gestational surrogacy can range from $75,000 to $100,000. Those costs are all-inclusive, covering all legal and medical costs, surrogate fees, agency fees, and insurance—all the numerous tasks of putting together a surrogacy and seeing it through.

An agency like Growing Generations will match prospective parents with a surrogate and/or an egg donor and will then manage the process—including, if desired, counseling. Halm says his staff works "with a handful of egg donor agencies," while the surrogates "come largely through word of mouth. Neighbors refer neighbors; sisters-in-law refer each other. There is even a surrogacy community on the Internet, and a lot happens in chat rooms." The agency is also plugged into a network of lawyers experienced in surrogacy and parental rights issues. In the first four years of its existence, Growing Generations helped some four hundred individuals. Halm estimates that at any one time, some 30 surrogates are pregnant or in the midst of the medical process, with another 30 clients on the waiting list.

Meanwhile, in the Simard-Halm household, "Luc was such an easy baby," says Marcellin, "that we forgot how tough Malina had been." The men began hankering after another baby in the house. This time, at long last, there was an agency they could go to that would find them a surrogate and an egg donor and even handle the legal issues, an agency that was very much their own—not just because Will worked at Growing Generations but because it existed to serve the gay community above all. Perhaps because the process was now so much easier, Will and Marcellin took advantage of the situation to add something new to the mix that would make it considerably tougher—that is, they decided to make this baby a girl. Why? "Malina wanted a sister," says Will, "and there are enough men in this house." So they tried to separate the X and Y chromosomes.

Says Dr. Simard: "There was an 80 percent chance it would work," so the men were excited when they went in to be present for the ultrasound. The doctor roamed across the grainy picture, then stopped suddenly and announced: "There it is. A penis!" Will nearly fell to the floor. They had been so sure of having a girl they had given away all of Luc's baby clothes. They went out and bought more for their son, Harlan—called Harley, their first Growing Generations baby, born in March 2002.

Being the fathers of three has changed both their lives. For Marcellin, the main breadwinner, "it is nice to be open about myself. As a cardiologist, I used to be professionally closeted. But as a father, I have to be out. The reaction has been very, very positive. Nobody was judgmental—not one doctor. Everybody has been totally supportive."

Will, who is the more stay-at-home parent, feels that as a man in what he calls "the female-centric parenting world," he is "received with reservation and some skepticism. I feel different being a man so involved in parenting. I go to Mommy and Me classes and sit in a circle with twelve women, and I sense that my presence makes them probably not as comfortable in these surroundings that are traditionally safe havens for mothers and their kids." He also identifies a "Mommy Mafia at school," one that keeps him from participating "as much as I'd like to." Still, "no one has ever said anything," and Will persists in being "very involved."

When Malina started school, Will hosted a "parent chat." "I invited all the parents of her classmates to a coffee at the school to talk about our family. Ninety percent of them showed up—both parents—and we explained how our family was created." There were two goals, Will says. "I wanted to establish that I had an open door for any questions they or their kids might raise about Malina and her family." And he wanted "to educate the parents themselves that it's possible not to have a mother." The concept, says Will, made a lot of jaws drop; after all, everybody has a mother, right? Wrong, Halm insists. "We have an egg donor and a surrogate. No mother."

Malina understands it. She "knows what a surrogate is," says Marcellin, "knows she grew in a woman's tummy, and knows that the possessor of the tummy is not her mommy." She also knows that her fathers went to a doctor to plant their seed in the woman's tummy, and she'd like to visit the doctor's office someday. Malina's classmates also accept the story, her fathers report—some are even jealous that she has a papa as well as a daddy—and now the classmates' parents accept it as well.

In addition to supportive classmates, friends, and neighbors, the Simard-Halm children have a large extended family. Will's mother lives with them and cooks their dinners most nights. Marcellin is the youngest of 20 children from a small town in Canada, so Malina, Luc, and Harley can claim about 50 French-speaking cousins in Quebec. What's more, all of the Simard-Halm surrogates remain family friends; two have served as godmothers to the children they delivered. As for biology, the children are "all Eurasian—biracial," says Will, "and how they got that way is nobody's business but ours—and, eventually, theirs." What counts, he says, is that "there is absolutely no difference in my love for the three kids. I don't even think about the issue." Says Marcellin: "I feel the same way."

But isn't the biological connection the main reason for pursuing surrogacy, as opposed to any other option? Well, first of all, "we have no judgments about a better way to make a family," says Halm. "We support all ways." And in fact, biology was not the driving force for Halm and Simard in choosing surrogacy; in their case, the motive was involvement in the process and a chance to exercise some control over it, as much control as fathers can.

But yes, most Growing Generations clients start off by saying they want a biological connection. Yet they don't end that way. From the intake and exit interviews that are routine at Growing Generations, agency staff have found that at the end of the process, when the family has been created and clients are asked what they liked about surrogacy, "they talk less about the biological connection than about the process, about meeting their wonderful surrogate, going through the pregnancy, the first ultrasound."

Simard and Halm believe that that appreciation of the process defines a profound value of surrogacy for gay men, although it is a value most gay men may not think of at first: the "advantage," as Will Halm defines it, "of being really involved in the pregnancy. It is pregnancy under the microscope. You know the surrogate from day one. You go through the process with her. It's a chance to be fully involved in the creation of your family."

In the end, Halm reports, for the men who become fathers through surrogacy, "the biological connection becomes unimportant. Since only one sperm can fertilize the egg and only one partner can be the biological dad, it just becomes a question of love, equal and shared."

Growing Pains

I n coming out as gay men, our generation had to give up the idea of parenthood," says Chuck Jones, father of two. "We were raised in the idea that gay men would never be fathers, and many of us substituted 'stuff' for not being able to be parents—designer dogs, showplace homes, careers. But a lot of it is so much transference for having to give up the traditional aspects of adulthood."

That is why parenthood, says Jones's partner, Richard Parker, "is transforming the gay community." Transforming it? How so? "We're growing up," says Parker. And he and Jones have the growing pains to prove it.

For Chuck Jones, the pain goes way back. Disinherited by his family for his sexuality and estranged from them, Jones has long had "a sense of emotional orphanhood." Result? "It was always important for me to be a parent."

When he and Parker became a couple in the early nineties, "we were both clear we wanted to be parents," Parker says; "we just didn't know how to go about it." They had moved to Santa Fe, a small city with a large number of same-sex households, and there they joined a gay parenting group, mostly to explore their options.

Surrogacy seemed risky; it would mean taking a large measure of responsibility for another human being during a process that can be destabilizing. In addition, says Chuck, "there were court cases at that time in which biological kids were being removed from the homes of gay parents." Besides, both men were middle-aged, established, and eager to *parent,* not necessarily to procreate. They turned to adoption, which was Chuck's original preference in any event.

Domestic adoption in New Mexico, however, would require two years of foster parenting—a long rehearsal for men in their forties. More to the point, they were told outright that, as gay men, they would be "at the bottom of the list." They had worries about domestic adoption, too—the fear that a birthparent might come back years later to reclaim an adopted child.

By a process of elimination, then, "international adoption seemed a very good option," says Chuck. What's more, the staff at an international adoption agency were "receptive and eager," even though—or perhaps because—Parker and Jones were their first gay male couple.

They went through the required procedures and answered hard

questions about the potential "problems" they would accept in a child. They said they preferred a two- to five-year-old, were open to siblings, would accept deafness, missing limbs, and heart defects. The agency matched them with a Russian two-year-old, Alex, who had sleeping problems and "an enlarged head." The enlarged head assessment, they learned, was possibly due to a different measuring system; a doctor who reviewed Alex's file said he looked fine, and the men concluded he had been put up for adoption because of financial hardship.

They said yes, and then they waited. Russian law requires the adoptive parent—Chuck, in this case—to appear in court before a judge, officials from the office of education, and the child's social worker–advocate. In addition, Russian law does not allow gay adoptions, so Chuck knew

he would need to closet himself to be approved as Alex's father. When the court date was set, he flew to Russia, then traveled to the orphanage—four hours from Moscow, on the border with Kazakhstan—to meet Alex.

The men had created a book about their house and had sent it to the orphanage months before, "to prepare Alex for Papa." When Chuck walked into the orphanage, Alex took one look, froze, then said: "Papa?" He then proceeded to hide behind an orphanage staff member, but eventually, he approached Chuck tentatively and soon was sitting on his lap. It was clear he had had "good treatment but not a lot of attention," Chuck says. He was nearly three, but mentally he was "less than a year old," according to Chuck, and his physical coordination was also underdeveloped: "He could barely walk three steps without falling down."

In court in Russia, Chuck "was grilled for three hours." They asked him a lot about the women in his life. Why wasn't he married? What did he expect of a wife? Where did his women relatives live? Chuck dissembled. He appropriated members of Richard's family and pretended they lived nearby. "The geography was a lie," he says, "but the emotional relationship was the truth."

Still, going back into the closet was hard for Chuck—very hard. "I came out at an early age," Chuck says, "and have always worked in the gay community. I have been described as 'beyond gay,' and the gay community has been my family. It was difficult to deny that. But when you feel so strongly that you need to make your family, you do what you need to do. By that time, we had had months to establish an emotional relationship with Alex. I had met him. He was our kid." Had he been asked outright about his sexuality, Chuck admits that he "would have lied."

Nine months after Chuck and Richard first filled out adoption application papers, the Russian court said yes, and that same day, Chuck went and got Alex at the orphanage. He "screamed and cried" as they drove away, but after three blocks, said "Papa?" and was then fine—at least as far as attachment was concerned.

Given Alex's level of development, however, Chuck "was in effect bringing home a really big infant." Alex was not toilet trained, and his means of communication consisted of some Russian baby talk and sign language. Yet those issues turned out to be the easy ones. What was tough was Alex's difficulty in walking, his poor socialization—"he would go into a corner," says Richard, "rock back and forth, and get a glazed look in his eyes"—and his inability to sleep. "He would sleep in fifteen-minute snatches, then wake up screaming. It was painful to see. He was so displaced, he didn't know where he was." His fathers would pick Alex up and walk him up and down the room till he slept again.

They loved him, they hugged him, and they learned to "let him be scared," says Chuck. They were all in the living room one day, and "Alex got really scared over something. And between the two of us, we realized we needed to let him go through that *with us present,* so that he could develop a level of trust." Gradually, it all worked. Alex learned to sleep, the screaming stopped, the fear abated.

When he had been with them a year and a half, Jones and Parker decided that Alex needed a brother. The second time around with the same agency, says Chuck, "it was easier than buying a car." Agency staff called with a match before the two men had finished filling out the application: this time, a two-year-old from Romania. The process took only four months; Richard, taking his turn at the experience, went overseas to bring their second son home. They named him Elvis, a fairly common name in eastern Europe, says Richard, and not uncommon in New Mexico, as it turns out. Elvis didn't speak much, "but he smiled a lot," says Richard, who became the adoptive father of record. When Richard brought Elvis home, Alex and Chuck were waiting for them at the airport. Alex had balloons for his new little brother, but Elvis didn't know what they were.

There were the usual adjustment pangs: Alex at first kept wondering out loud when Elvis was "going back to Romania," and Chuck and Richard found themselves adapting to a new personality. "Elvis is a power broker," says Chuck. "Where Alex survived by going into a corner, Elvis survived by manipulating other people. He had been the pet of all the caregivers in the orphanage, and we can see it. He's very honest and genuine."

In time, the four of them became a family—officially as well as emotionally. In fact, both boys were adopted three times: by one of their fathers in their native countries, then again by the adoptive father back home in the States, and a third time by the other father as a second-parent adoption.

Although the agency had given the men as much information about both boys as was possible, Chuck and Richard are convinced that what they know, which is meager enough, is questionable. "These are remote, impoverished areas of the world," Chuck explains, "and people there put their kids in orphanages because they are poor. But because there are extreme taboos around adoption, they may well give false information about parentage and background." Parker and Jones took the attitude "that we would have as much control over who our kids are as we would if we were pregnant. We would open ourselves to the process, and the child who came to us in that way would be our child. Is that any different from the way any biological parents get their family? They are nobody's kids but ours, and while I'd like a lot of information about their backgrounds, I also really don't care."

Besides, time and growth in a family environment have had their impact. Alex has made "major physical progress," says Richard. "Once he began to develop motor skills, he excelled at them," becoming a coordinated, dexterous, talented, and self-confident athlete. He has been catching up in occupational and communications skills as well, dealing with auditory dyslexia and with the consequences of that early lack of sensory stimulation.

Elvis is the reverse of his brother. He has shown no problems learning but still needs to do some physical catching up. He is also a different personality—"headstrong," Richard calls him, "but also cute and charming when he wants to be." The two brothers "get along famously," Richard goes on. "They're a very strong unit. When they fight or compete, we try to steer it back to them and stay out of it. Alex is bigger and older, and Elvis is diminutive for his age but crafty, which frustrates Alex."

The boys call both fathers Daddy, or they call them Richard and Chuck, or, "when they're being silly and baby-ish," they call them "Mommy," or they call them Daddy and The Other Daddy. "We haven't dictated what they should call us," say Parker and Jones.

They are a family that golfs together. Family time is mandated as well as cherished. Richard is a dentist—the first "out" medical provider in Santa Fe, Chuck says—and Chuck, a onetime psychotherapist, manages Richard's dental office, but Parker and Jones also "try to make sure we have daily time as a family in our home," says Chuck. "For the kids' sake, we want them to know this is their space.

"And I need to have a home," Chuck adds. "Part of having a family is to regenerate that part of me that prizes the relationships that remain

eternal. Being home together after school and on weekends is important. My strongest desire is to be a full-time dad."

Sometimes, says Richard, "it feels like there's a presumption that men cannot be nurturing. It's just assumed that women nurture, so there's the implication that lesbians are automatically ready for parenting. But gay men have a struggle to assert themselves as viable parents." Adds Chuck: "Support systems are not readily available to us. People certainly do support us, but they don't get involved in our lives. So we have had to be creative, make something out of nothing, make conscious efforts to create support systems on our own."

Richard defines the support they do receive: "A lot of people love the fact that we're these very out gay men who have started a family and remained out and are still active in the community. But we don't go to the gallery openings every Friday night anymore, don't go to the opera as much as we used to, and our conversation topics have changed."

So while both men remain "very involved" in the gay community and have become "the gay poster dads in town," in Chuck's phrase, their "circle of friends has changed dramatically," and they find themselves somewhat isolated from the gay community. Instead, their friends now tend to be straight couples who are the parents of their kids' friends. "We've struggled socially since becoming parents," Chuck says. "It's been hard. A lot of our gay male friends have pushed us away. I think our being parents brings up unresolved issues that gay men don't let themselves consider. That's why they don't invite us to dinner anymore; it puts a mirror up to them reminding them of issues they'd rather not face." And Richard suspects that many of their gay friends "don't know what to do with us or how to act around kids."

Whatever the reasons, where once "pretty much all our friends were gay and lesbian," says Richard, "now some of our best friends are heterosexual, and we are often the only gay couple around."

Their isolation from the gay community pulls a leg of support out from under them when it's most needed. "You can joke about same-sex couples not getting pregnant accidentally," Chuck goes on, "but in fact, the joke hints at how conscious our effort to have children must be. Gay men can't assume anything. To become parents, we have to overcome the barriers as gay men, then take on even more. It *is* hard."

Then why do it? Why take on the effort? Because it's worth it. Because gay men today don't have to give up the idea of parenthood, and Parker and Jones are living proof. Because it is making Richard and

Chuck "grow up" and because it can "bring a broader dimension to the gay community than just gentrifying another neighborhood." Because "we wanted there to be something beyond ourselves," in Richard Parker's words. Because "once you bring children into your life," Chuck says, "you bring depth into your day-to-day existence—exponentially."

Positive Signs

At his baptism, Nicky Hosterman, then not quite three months old, kept moving his hands. Most people assumed this was normal baby babble and that Nicky, not surprisingly, was *signing* the babble. Not surprisingly because one of Nicky's two fathers, Eric Littles, is completely deaf, and since Eric is the stay-at-home dad, signing is the form of communication Nicky recognizes best—even at his tender age.

Nicky's other father is John Hosterman. He and Eric had been together six and a half years when they adopted Nicholas. The two met at the small dinner party of a mutual friend, dated for a few years, then moved in together in a suburb of Chicago. At the time, Eric, who is

African-American, was working at a bank; Hosterman, who is white, was and still is a learning disabilities specialist with a private practice. The two bought a house and acquired two cats. What was left, Eric quipped, but to have children?

And in fact, both had always wanted children; they just never thought it was possible. Eric was particularly keen on having biological children. "I wanted a child that would come from my body," he says, one that could "make a new generation for my family's pride." Confronted by the legal issues, however, and given the fact that the two lacked a circle of women friends that might include a potential surrogate, Eric finally relinquished that idea.

There were family pressures on Eric not to have a child at all. Profoundly religious Baptists, most of the members of his family initially had "a very hard time," in Eric's words, with his sexuality and his partnership with John—in fact, "with everything we do." When it came to the idea of gay dads, their line was that children need a mother. As to the adoption option, which the two men considered next, a sister warned Eric "that gay adoption was a bad idea because children who have same-sex parents would be bothered and harassed and picked on by their classmates in school." To these pressures, however, as to most of his family's disapproval, Eric "didn't really pay much attention."

His family's displeasure was countered by what John and Eric learned from talking with other gay parents and especially from the 2001 Family Week they attended in Saugatuck, Michigan. Sponsored by COLAGE and the Family Pride Coalition, Family Week is seven days of workshops, seminars, and activities; the year Littles and Hosterman went, it drew some 40 to 55 families—two-hundred-plus people. Seeing all the children and families in action at Family Week, plus all the things he learned and all the advice he received, convinced Eric "to go ahead and adopt a baby."

But if adoption seemed the most viable option, there was actually a lot more to it than just viability. John Hosterman is adopted, and, he says, "having been adopted makes me proadoption." Hosterman has always been close to his adoptive family, but when he was in college, he felt the need to search for his biological parents. His adoptive parents told him about the Connecticut-based agency through which they had found him, and a social worker was able to identify and locate John's birthmother. Tentatively at first, John and his mother, Darlene, exchanged letters through the agency. Then they began an email correspondence. And finally, in January 1998, they arranged to meet.

"I flew to Albany, New York," Hosterman recalls. "It was very emotional for both of us. We spent a couple of days." The woman who had placed John as an unwed mother was now the long-married mother of two other sons. Yet she and John "hit it off immediately. We forged an instant bond. We had similar likes and dislikes, and it just felt like we had known each other for years." The two have remained in close touch; they email one another every other day or so and are often together on holidays.

One has the sense that John Hosterman feels that his adoption has enriched his life, that having both a birth family and an adoptive family doubles the fullness of his existence. "I have no bitterness about having been adopted," he says. "I had a wonderful childhood, and I have a wonderful family. And now I have a wonderful addition to my life with Darlene and her family." He sums it up: "I lost nothing, missed nothing, sacrificed nothing" by being adopted. "And I think it is wonderful that Nicholas is adopted, too."

But it didn't happen right away.

The two had been together five years when they began seriously to pursue the idea of adoption. They logged onto the Web to search for local agencies, to find possible nearby adoptive parents who had already gone through the experience, and to locate organizations and resources in the Chicago area. The search yielded both official facts and word-of-mouth information, and "all paths," says John Hosterman, "seemed to lead to an agency in Oak Park," one of only two in the area, as far as the two men could determine, that were open to dealing with same-sex couples. That is where Hosterman and Littles went in the summer of 2000.

They filled out the paperwork and did the homestudy. Agency staff warned them that "no" birthmother would choose a gay couple, so they would have to wait for an abandoned baby—and it might be a long wait. They were prepared for that. The two men had also been "kind of picky" about what they wanted—specifically, a healthy, biracial boy. They had "gone through a long process and knew exactly what we wanted," so when they were offered a number of babies who "tended to be not what we wanted," they held firm. "We were given lots of encouragement," John says, "but no baby."

In September 2001, just about a year after they began the process, the agency ate its words of warning and was able to match them with a birthmother who was "okay" about a same-sex adoptive couple. John and Eric did not meet the woman, but they received "some background information" on her and were asked to pay many of her expenses from then until her due date in October.

"October came and went," John says, "and there were lots of excuses." Maybe she had miscalculated the date of conception; maybe she had counted wrong; maybe she was having twins and wasn't really that far along in the pregnancy after all. Then, says Hosterman, "November came and went. December came and went. We were pretty frantic over Christmas and New Year's; we had abandoned all our holiday plans in anticipation of a baby." In fact, the idea of twins was looking more likely—"she was so enormous," says John.

The mystery was revealed shortly after the new year. It was simple: the birthmother had decamped to Indiana. Her baby had been born, and she had skipped town. Call it a novel variation on an old theme, an innovative wrinkle on how to swindle somebody. What irked Hosterman and Littles was that the woman, in John's words, "had a rap sheet a mile long with the Department of Children and Family Services" (DCFS), and their adoption agency simply hadn't investigated her thoroughly

enough—if at all. "There was some indication," John says, "that she had had significant problems with previous children. She had used various aliases as well." And DCFS was certainly not pleased to hear that she was giving birth to yet another child while she was "in danger of losing others."

Having been "strung along for four months" only to have their hopes brutally dashed, Eric and John were very, very disappointed. "We had spent four months emotionally tied up with this," John says. And he adds simply: "We got screwed."

Three days later, the agency called and said a birthmother again "had chosen us from a whole array of couples"—the very thing the agency had assured them could never happen. The brother of the woman in question was a gay man who, with his partner, already had children. The woman had hoped her brother could take her baby, but he couldn't manage it, so she was looking for "a similar case," John says. She herself had another child, an elderly and sick mother, and "significant personal problems"; a second child would be too much for her to manage. She was Caucasian and said the birthfather was African-American. For everyone involved, it seemed a perfect match. What's more, the mother was eight months pregnant at the time.

The baby came two weeks early—and was delivered by C-section. John and Eric raced to the hospital, where the hospital social worker blocked the birthmother's request for the two men to be in the delivery room and "didn't even want us to see the baby after the birth." It was unpleasant, to say the least, to confront this kind of homophobia at such a time and in such a place. "Fortunately," says Hosterman, the birthmom, whom they met for the first time in the hospital, was adamant that they be allowed to see and spend time with their son.

In a clichéd near-parody of expectant fatherhood, the two fathers-to-be paced in the waiting room. Nicholas weighed in at nine and a half pounds at birth. Warding off the hospital social worker's arguments, the birthmother signed the papers relinquishing her rights to the baby even before the 72-hour waiting period was up. "She was solid in her decision," John says. "She did not want her baby in even temporary foster care. She saw and held him, then signed away her rights." John became Nicholas's legal guardian, with adoption to follow after six months, and a second-parent adoption by Eric to be concluded through the courts.

At the birthmother's request, there has been no contact with her since Nicky's birth, although Eric and John have agreed to forward letters and photos every three months for the first year and once a year thereafter. No one is more respectful of her, of her decision, and of "the difficulties she went through" than John Hosterman. "I intend to make sure that Nicholas understands all this when he's older," John says.

Meanwhile, Eric, John, and Nicholas came home. At first, says John, "we didn't really know what we were doing." They had taken some classes in caring for a baby but, like most new parents, still felt somewhat inadequate. Yet, like most new parents, they "muddled through," in John's words. Fortunately, Nicky's infancy "was not too complicated. He slept a lot and took the bottle easily." And the two men quickly "got the hang of diapers."

Of course, it was a time of great joy. The only odd thing was that Nicky did not at all appear to be *bi*racial. "He is pretty light-skinned," says John; "he is certainly not *half*-black"—despite what the birthmother claimed. It means that Nicky does not particularly look like either of them, but of course that "does not matter because he is ours now," as John says.

They live in an extremely diverse community, a place where being an interracial couple and having an adopted baby is not an issue. Or rather, when it is an issue, it is one that elicits "really positive feedback." Their immediate neighborhood, for example, includes white, black, Filipino, and Pakistani neighbors, all of whom got together to throw a baby shower for Eric and John before Nicky's birth and to host a party to meet the baby once he arrived.

The two men's families have also gathered around—except for Eric's father, divorced from his mother, who still "won't be in the same room with John and won't have anything to do with the baby." Says Eric of his father: "He can explain himself to God." Still, between Eric's mother and sisters and John's two families—biological and adoptive—Nicky has a pretty big extended family, not to mention three grandmothers. He has already enjoyed an annual vacation with one of those grandmothers and the rest of the Hostermans, John's adoptive family. And Darlene, John's birthmother, although of a rather conservative bent, has really made John, Eric, and Nicky "part of her family," all of whom have showered Nicholas with "tons of gifts and cards." The same goes for Eric's mother and two sisters, who have been "great," say both dads.

Eric quit his job in the mortgage department of the bank to become a stay-at-home father, and while John often works from home, it is Eric who is the primary, full-time caregiver. Since he is and always has been totally deaf, the house has been rigged with lamps everywhere. The doorbell, the phone, the smoke alarm, the baby-cry sensor: all make varicolored lights flash at different rates so that Eric can distinguish among them. In his eyes, as for any parent, there is a big difference between the "sound" of the doorbell and his son's crying. It all "works perfectly," says John.

Eric enjoys "being a stay-at-home father and taking good care of Nicholas," although he complains he has gained weight. He swears by *The Contented Little Baby,* by the Englishwoman Gina Ford, an experienced maternity nurse who favors establishing a daily routine and offers tips for getting a newborn to sleep through the night by 10 weeks. Nicky must be a fast learner because he managed the feat at seven weeks.

Theirs is what any hearing person would call a quiet house. "Occasionally, I use my indistinct voice to call the baby's name," Eric says, "but I usually use sign language to communicate with Nicholas." And although the house is mostly free of the sounds of radios chattering or music playing, "Nicholas likes to hear John's voice," Eric goes on, "and he likes to watch children's videotapes on TV, especially 'Sing and Sign,' " tapes that teach kids both the words of songs and how to sign the words.

Certainly, Nicholas will be bilingual. In fact, says John, who also signs fluently, "he may learn sign language earlier than spoken English," since it is, in effect, the primary language of his household. "He becomes very animated when he watches the *Sing and Sign* videos, and he reacts to signing as well as to voiced English. It's the same smile when you come into the room whether you say or sign 'What a good boy!' " Both fathers are thrilled with this development. "Research shows," John says, "that kids can learn more than one language, and that if they don't, that part of the brain shuts down or is used for something else." That won't be an issue for their Nicky. He'll communicate silently or aloud—to two fathers who can't wait to hear what he has to say.

A Winning Fight

I think sometimes gay people are afraid to fight and push," says Kevin Williams. "They're afraid to hold public agencies accountable."

It is not a fear to which Williams or his partner, Tim Eustace, have ever fallen prey.

"We're famous for being advocates for our children," Eustace says. "Where our kids are concerned, we have the reputation of being a pain in the ass."

Eustace and Williams have waged their battles on behalf of their children from yet another classic American suburb—Maywood, New Jersey, a town of tree-lined streets, with a small but diverse population, just minutes from New York City. It's the kind of place where the head of the Chamber of Commerce is also likely to serve on the borough council, be an active member of the church and the Rotary Club, and participate in the town's annual 5K foot race. That's an exact description of Tim Eustace, a chiropractor by profession and a political activist by avocation. Williams, the stay-at-home parent, is a onetime psychiatric social worker who now does couples counseling and consults on issues of gay adoption.

A couple since 1978, Eustace and Williams are both white. Their two sons are African-American. Both were born HIV-positive to a cocaine-using mother—Kyle in 1988 and Corey in 1993. A third son, Lee, also African-American, died of AIDS in 1991 at the age of twelve. A portrait of Lee now hangs proudly in the very same elementary school that threw him out twice in response to parents' fears of his disease. To repeat: a classic American suburb.

In 1988, when Tim and Kevin had been a couple for a decade, they became the first openly gay couple to apply to the state to become adoptive parents. "They didn't know what to do with us," Kevin says of the state's child welfare staff. "Our social worker told us she had never met a gay person and thought one of us would show up in a dress. We were asked two questions: 'Will you tell the children they're adopted?' and 'Will you breast-feed?' "

But to the state Division of Youth and Family Services (DYFS), which was desperate to place boarder babies—especially those born HIV-positive—the Eustace-Williams's willingness, in Kevin's words, to "adopt kids who are unwanted by anyone else" was a godsend. Later—much later—a hardened and cynical social worker in the state system admitted to Kevin that in placing "AIDS kids" with gay parents, the state believed it was unloading a problem with the least effort. Said the social worker: "They consider they're giving trash to the trash." Eustace and Williams may have suspected as much in 1988, but it didn't particularly surprise them, and it certainly didn't stop them. "For our kids," Kevin says, "the choices were institutionalization or a loving home." The family they became is the ultimate rebuke to the state's dismissive indifference.

The two went through all the required procedures for becoming adoptive parents—training, fingerprinting, home inspection—and were advised they could expect to hear something "in a year or so." The next morning, their phone rang; DYFS needed to place a baby born HIV-positive. Were Eustace and Williams interested? They were not only interested, they were "thrilled," says Tim Eustace. "And," he adds in an understatement, "our lives changed" that morning.

They changed even more that afternoon. That's when DYFS called back to ask for help with what they called "a problem." An eight-year-old who had just tested positive for AIDS had been thrown out of the foster home where he had been for five years. Could Tim and Kevin make room for him—temporarily? The state gave the men five minutes to decide. They did it in one.

Eight-year-old Lee arrived the next day, bringing with him "two bags of dirty clothing, his entire worldly possessions," says Tim. He went "from a poor inner-city neighborhood, where he referred to himself as 'colored,' to a middle-class suburb with two white gay guys." Even billed as temporary, this qualified as a radical change.

It was a radical change for Eustace and Williams, too. Their four-bedroom house was spacious, but nothing about it was ready for children—and certainly not for a newborn. Thankfully, they had a week before the newborn, Kyle, was to be released from the hospital. Tim's sister-in-law hastily arranged a baby shower for some 25 guests, and a number of local dignitaries also showed up. Everyone brought something

for eight-year-old Lee, and as for Kyle, as Tim recalls, they "didn't have to buy baby clothes for two years."

Still, to morph in one week into the parents of an eight-year-old and an infant was, in Kevin's words, "pretty bizarre. One night it was 'Dollar Night' at the local gay bar in nearby Hackensack. A week later, I'm baking cupcakes for the PTA."

And the morphing was not entirely smooth. There were some nasty phone messages and a few pieces of hate mail. As the only black kid in his class, Lee went through a rough adjustment that ranged from verbal insults to physical attacks—and not only because of his color. One day he came home and said "Daddy Kevin, would you sleep on the couch?"

"On the couch? Why?"

"The kids in school say my parents are gay," came the answer. "And if you sleep on the couch, you won't be gay."

"Well," Kevin wondered, "why not ask Daddy Tim to sleep on the couch?"

Said Lee: "Because he's a real doctor, and you're just a social worker."

There was a time when the social worker had thought that "quitting a private practice of 36 patients to be home all day would be easy. But this was a huge transition to a 24/7 job. I remember actually falling asleep while eating a pizza. The next week, I fell ill with pneumonia. It was rough."

It grew even rougher when the local school board kicked Lee out of school because he had AIDS. "The first time it happened," Tim recalls, "we called a public hearing with an expert on pediatric AIDS as the main speaker. Our aim was to quell fears. And we also wanted people to know we weren't going anywhere. The next time it happened, the New Jersey Supreme Court had handed down its decision,* so we threatened to take the school board to court." That did it; the expulsions stopped. The disease, however, kept going.

And Eustace and Williams kept fighting. They fought to get Lee on AZT, an early anti-AIDS drug—according to his doctor, he was the first child for whom it was prescribed. They fought to put him on a pain control program—another first. By the summer of 1990, when Lee was no longer able to eat, they fed him intravenously overnight so that he could

---

*The Court affirmed that people with AIDS were covered by the Americans with Disabilities Act and thus were entitled to "equality of opportunity, full participation, independent living, and economic self-sufficiency," as the Act proclaims—that is, they could not be isolated or discriminated against on the basis of their disease.

continue to go to school throughout the fall of 1990 and into the winter of 1991. Every other week, Kevin took him into the hospital for a blood transfusion. Usually the transfusion meant an overnight hospital stay, but one week, the transfusion was scheduled for the day before school pictures were to be taken. Lee was desperate to be there for the picture, surely his last, so Kevin said "no" to the usual requirement that Lee stay overnight, and when the hospital wouldn't release the boy, "I signed him out," Kevin recalls. An enraged physician confronted Kevin in front of his son. "Who the fuck do you think you are?" he shouted. "I'm putting you down for child abuse for removing this child from my care." And he did, filing an accusation with DYFS. But Lee was in school the next day for the photo session.

In February 1991, Lee had to stop going to school. Instead, his classmates came to visit, and a multilayered circle of support—family, friends, neighbors, church members—rallied around the household. Tim and Kevin had prepared themselves for Lee's death since he had come into their lives, or so they thought, but preparation did not keep the pain at bay. "We learned so much from him," says Kevin, his voice breaking. "He had a lot of friends. He was a Mets fan."

Lee died on March 26, 1991. The next day, Kevin was exonerated of the child abuse accusation, and the doctor who filed the accusation was sanctioned. "We had won the battle of blood transfusions at our hospital," Tim says with an edge of bitterness.

Although Kyle missed his brother achingly, he flourished—partly, no doubt, because his parents fought for him to flourish. As an HIV-positive infant, he was part of an AIDS study at a time when doctors "suited up in spacesuits with masks and gloves and boots to examine him," says Tim.

"I'd be standing in the room normally dressed. And the doctors would say, 'Typically, the parents leave now.' And I'd say, 'I'm sure they do.' And I'd just stay there, be there, while they strapped him down and gave him needles."

Kyle's HIV-positive status meant they couldn't buy health insurance for him, either. Eustace and Williams went to court to fight for medical coverage. They were zealous, aggressive advocates before a judge who was appalled at the situation. They got the coverage.

So it may not have been solely for clinical reasons that Kyle's condition converted to HIV-negative status by the age of two,* as Lee was growing sicker and sicker. "The hardest thing," says Kevin, "was telling Lee that Kyle was HIV-negative. He was so loving toward his little brother." In a way, Kyle's new healthy status was a double-edged sword that held some fear for Eustace and Williams. "I thought," says Tim, "that if Kyle were HIV-negative, they wouldn't let us adopt"—that the state would find more "appropriate" parents for this now healthy boy.

In 1993, Eustace and Williams learned that Kyle's mother had given birth to a boy who had been placed for adoption without the Eustace-Williamses being notified. That is contrary to DYFS's own regulations requiring that the adoptive parents of a child's sibling or siblings have the first right of refusal for the child. Eustace and Williams protested—vocally and vigorously—and a report was ordered. "We spent six months gnashing our teeth in anguish," says Tim. When the report was issued, it concluded that "nothing wrong had been done" by anyone at the agency;

*Babies are born with their mother's immune system. Most babies born to HIV-positive mothers convert to negative when their own immune systems kick in.

at the same time, Tim and Kevin were told, sub rosa, to "wait a month and you'll get what you want." They waited, and they got Corey, and no social worker in the state system ever got a rap on the knuckles or a reprimand or a demerit on his or her personnel file for directly violating agency standards. "The coverup is disgusting," Kevin says, "but we don't care."

"You have to pick your battles," says Tim. "We had let them know we were ready to push. If we thought we could stop the state's racism and homophobia, we'd be nuts. We wanted to push the sibling issue because it was their own regulation they were violating, but we wanted our child. We won the battle we wanted to win."

Corey, also born HIV-positive, also converted to negative status by the age of two. Neither he nor Kyle has ever experienced in school the kind of trouble that beset their late older brother. Kyle plays baseball, soccer, and heavy-metal guitar. Corey is obsessed by the sinking of the *Titanic* and the attack on Pearl Harbor. Kyle has been to two presidential inaugurations, and both boys have been to Congressional swearings-in. Tim and the boys ski every winter; while he and Corey are doing half-pipes on the mountaintop, Kyle has graduated to snowboarding and is very, very cool. Kyle and Corey know they are siblings, and they keep a photograph of their mother.

Their fathers pay ample attention to their sons' race and African-American heritage—with books, discussion, a planned trip to Africa. "We may even overdo it," says Tim. The boys are proud of their blackness. Corey jokes that his parents have to wear suntan lotion; he doesn't.

Kyle and Corey are as civic-minded as their parents. They march with the Rotary Club and know what's going on in the borough council.

They are part of the fabric of their community. They are also the children of gay parents who live their lives proudly and in public. The boys were there when Tim and Kevin were married in the Episcopal Church, and they accompanied their fathers on their honeymoon cruise in Alaska. When Tim and Kevin sat down with the boys' teachers to discuss the issue of their sons' having two fathers, the teachers said: "What makes you think you're the only gay couple with kids in this school?"

For all the fighting they have done for their children, Eustace and Williams know there will be fights the boys will have to wage on their own. "Adopted kids carry their own baggage," says Kevin, who then concedes that all kids carry baggage of some sort. Still, he and Tim worry. They worry about the cocoon of their neighborhood in Maywood, a place so idyllic people jokingly call it Mayberry. In Maywood, the Eustace-Williams family is bathed in genuine and widespread support—"and the people who don't approve of us tend to keep quiet or be shunned," says Tim. What happens when the boys emerge from the cocoon, when they confront the realities of being a black boy and then a black man in America? When Kyle got his driver's license in the state in which racial profiling by highway police most dramatically engaged the public consciousness, his parents worried. They worry when they think about their sons going on to high school and college and being "tested for their blackness, or for having gay white parents," says Tim. But then he answers his own worry. "Of course they'll have problems. Who doesn't? Should we outlaw parenthood for anybody who doesn't have problems? Kids with glasses have problems, kids with fat parents have problems, kids with stuffy parents have problems."

One Halloween, some kids in idyllic Maywood painted a swastika on a wall and drove past the Eustace-Williams house shouting "Niggers and faggots out!" The boys were equal parts indignant and afraid. Kyle went to the judge and reported the matter. The bigoted kids were fined for harassment. The incident has not been repeated. It would seem that knowing when and how to fight is a lesson the Eustace-Williams children learned at their fathers' knees.

Three's Company

For would-be fathers like James Garcia and Jon Langbert, the beauty and the burden of surrogacy are that you are plunged immediately into a relationship—at once awkwardly intimate and oddly distant—with a total stranger. The care and feeding of that relationship—literally as well as figuratively—can be as emotionally exacting for the fathers as pregnancy is physically demanding on the surrogate. For Jon and James, it was a roller-coaster ride from start to finish. Yet the result was so beyond their expectations and their wildest dreams as to be almost immeasurable. *Almost* immeasurable. The figure 3 would do: triplets Chaucer, Carter, and Tosca Garcia-Langbert.

Garcia, a graphic designer, and Langbert, an entrepreneur, came together in Texas in 1995 and in 1999 moved to New York where Jon was starting up an Internet business. It was during that summer before the move, James recalls, that they began to talk seriously about having children. For James, some sort of biological tie was important. "Family is particularly important in the Latino culture in which I've been raised," he says. "It's important for a part of me to go on, my name and my blood." In fact, his first choice for a surrogate was his sister. When that idea was roundly nixed by his brother-in-law, the two men "started doing some homework," says Jon, and found Growing Generations. At the time, of course, the two men could have had no idea how prophetic the agency's name would turn out to be. They asked for an information packet from the agency, liked what they saw, and made an appointment to fly out to California to meet with Growing Generations staff and to interview and be interviewed by various parties to the surrogacy process. James was 25 at the time, and Jon was 34.

"We were nervous about the interview," James concedes. "We wanted to be parent-worthy." But when a fertility doctor asked the two men why they wanted to be fathers, "it made me uncomfortable," James says. "My sister had kids, and nobody had asked her or my brother-in-law why they wanted to be parents. I felt I had as deserving a shot as anybody at parenthood." What particularly surprised James was that the individual asking the question was himself gay—and a fertility doctor.

"We signed on with Growing Generations," James goes on, "and committed to that working relationship." They were placed on a waiting list, were asked to complete a hefty paperwork package—all sorts of questionnaires plus a personal profile detailing who they were, why they wanted to be parents, why they chose surrogacy, and how they saw themselves working with a surrogate—and were told not to expect anything for at least six months.

Four months later, a staff member at Growing Generations phoned them to say that the agency had not yet received their personal profile—could Garcia and Langbert please send it along posthaste. They FedExed it overnight, suspecting—rightly—that the agency had found them a match. The next day, the agency called to confirm that Garcia and Langbert were "jumping up the list," in Jon's words. The surrogate in question had become uncomfortable that another couple with whom the agency had matched her were not fully "out" to their families. She wanted to be a surrogate for a gay couple, but she wanted everything about the process to be open.

This was the break that moved Garcia and Langbert up the list. The next step was to meet with her and her husband and arrange the deal. "We wanted," says Jon, "to settle everything on one trip." The men flew back to California.

Growing Generations drafted their contract with the surrogate. In it, says James, "everything is spelled out." By "everything" is meant the responsibilities of the parties, limitations and reservations, the expenses to be covered, and so forth. Central to the contract was a clause affirming that because this was her body, the surrogate had the final say on what she would and would not do. As for the finances, "you prefund your account for the entire process," says Jon, "a trust fund that Growing Generations administers, paying the bills out of that account as needed." In their case, as it happened, the multiple birth and attendant complications would "max out" their contract, and additional payments would be needed. But all that was still in the future.

At the time, their main concern was choosing an egg donor from a website "album." They looked at physical description, family history, and longevity, and tried to discern intelligence from what they saw and read. In the end, they went with a woman who had been through the process before.

With all the parties lined up, it was a matter of setting a target date for the transfer. First, both donor and surrogate were administered medication "to synchronize their cycles and increase egg production," as Jon explains it. "At the same time," he says, "we had to be checked out for sperm quality." Everything had to be carefully coordinated—especially

since the egg donor was coming from one place, the fathers from another, and the surrogate from yet a third location. On the appointed day, however, all the players arrived at the fertility clinic for the transfer.

As anonymous as things were supposed to be, James was "very nervous about running into the egg donor" as he and Jon moved around the clinic. The two were shown into a room "with an old TV and only straight porn videos," James says, and were instructed to "shoot fresh sperm for the eggs being harvested down the hall," as Jon recalls it. The result was eight embryos; the four best were chosen for implantation in the surrogate, while the others were frozen. "We saw 'our kids' as seven-cell creatures," James recalls, remembering how the embryonic cells had looked under the microscope before they were implanted.

But just a few days before implantation, there was a sudden hitch—one that threatened to put the kibosh on the whole process. The surrogate had gone to a Growing Generations retreat where she had become acquainted with a woman pregnant with twins. The woman was "enormous," in the surrogate's word, and she was uncomfortable. It had made the surrogate herself wary of a multiple pregnancy, and she now decided she wanted only three embryos transferred, not the originally agreed-on four that would increase the chances of a successful pregnancy.

A meeting was arranged—Jon and James, the surrogate, senior representatives from Growing Generations, and the fertility doctor. The doctor tried to assure the surrogate that the chances of twins were very slim and of triplets virtually nil. "Four embryos," he said, "is a good number." He had used four often in the past and had never gotten triplets. His confident tone of authority worked, and the surrogate yielded. As a final safeguard, the contract was amended to read that in the unlikely event of triplets, there would be selective reduction of one of the embryos. Jon and James, who had feared the whole deal might fall apart, breathed a sigh of relief.

Four embryos were duly implanted. Jon and James spent four days with the surrogate attending to her needs so she could have complete bed rest. Then she went home to the Midwest, and Langbert and Garcia flew back to Manhattan to wait.

They had bought the surrogate a home pregnancy test kit. One of its tests measured, inexactly, a multiple pregnancy, and over the next weeks, she reported to them that it was beginning to look like she might be pregnant with twins. Her first ultrasound, scheduled for a day when neither Jon nor James could fly out for it, would determine if she was pregnant and, if so, whether she was pregnant with twins.

There was a message on the Garcia-Langbert answering machine when James got home that night. Their surrogate. "Please call me," she said. James caught a trill of pent-up anxiety in her voice, and his own antennae began to vibrate with concern. When he finally got through to her on the phone, she asked if Jon were there as well. "I have to speak to both of you," she said, and the trill seemed to James to have gone up a pitch. With a range of worries going through his head—was she pregnant? was she healthy? was there a problem?—he managed to set up a three-way call. This time, the surrogate could not hold back her crying. "There are three of them," she said, "and I am really upset."

"We freaked out," says James. What should have been a moment of joy was, instead, "devastating." According to that last emendation of the contract, they might now have to perform selective reduction—something no one wanted to do, not the surrogate, not Jon and James. They also worried that the procedure might jeopardize the pregnancy altogether. The fertility doctor suggested that the surrogate's body might "naturally reduce" the number of embryos and recommended that everybody wait for the next ultrasound at 12 weeks. But at 12 weeks, says James, "you can see the babies forming"; if they were going to selectively reduce, let it at least be now.

Garcia and Langbert flew to the surrogate's home for a consult with a specialist in high-risk pregnancies. They were sensitive to the struggle she was going through: any multiple birth is risky; she would require a C-section; and the births would be two months premature. Certainly, this was a lot more than she had bargained for. And the care of her own children as well as concern over her health weighed heavily on her mind. They left the specialist's office, and the surrogate's husband said to come by the next day, that "he and his wife would have a decision for us."

But over breakfast the next morning, the subject never came up. Nor did it at lunch. At the airport, no one said a word. When the moment came for Jon and James to board the plane, "we all hugged each other and said good-bye," James recalls, "expecting that she would give us an answer or some indication of an answer." But there was none. The men flew home.

They knew this was her decision and no one else's—legally and logically. But the waiting game was hard. In their fear and agitation, Jon and James found themselves snapping at one another. That night, exhausted from their trip and worn out by their emotions, James called the surrogate's home. She had gone to bed, her husband said. The two men waited some more. Over the phone the next day, their surrogate finally confirmed that she would continue with the pregnancy and not selectively reduce.

But this hardly meant that Jon and James were home free. The health and well-being of the surrogate continued to affect their own health and

well-being. They worried about the pregnancy, the birth, the babies to come. When the surrogate decided to fly to a family funeral, "we were nervous wrecks," but they feared opposing the surrogate and damaging the relationship. It was a frustrating time.

They worked out some of the frustration by moving into a bigger apartment, shopping for baby furniture, researching child-rearing. As soon as they knew the sexes of the babies—two girls and a boy—friends threw them a baby shower at which the guests brought presents "in triplicate," Jon says.

December 2000: Jon and James flew to James's parents' home in Texas for the holidays. The pregnancy was nearing the end of month five, and the men were aware that the birth could come at any time. It was 6:00 A.M.

Christmas morning when James's mother knocked on their door. Their surrogate was in labor.

Jon, James, and James's mother arrived just as the babies were born that Christmas day. "The hospital personnel go by letter, not by names," says Jon, "so we gave them their names alphabetically as they came out." Baby A, a girl, was Chaucer; B for boy was Carter, their only son, and Baby C was Tosca. All three went immediately to the neonatal intensive care unit, where they remained for two and a half weeks; they spent another week in special care. While Jon flew back and forth, James was there the whole time—"the longest four weeks of my life," he says.

They stayed in the Ronald McDonald House across from the hospital. "It was snowing and miserable the whole time," James recalls. And they were stuck there. As confirmed Manhattanites, neither of them had driven a car in years. Not that there was anyplace to go; they wanted to be with their children.

"All were less than four pounds at birth," says Jon. "They had multiple wires coming in and out. It was quite a production for the nurse to put them on you. You were always afraid you'd squish them or mess up a tube or IV wire." The men "could hold them but couldn't handle them," James recalls. "They had no body fat. These kids were so small, so frail. And they couldn't suck, of course." Little by little over the four weeks, however, they grew fatter, stronger, more capable. Still, when they all finally went home, "a nurse flew with us," Jon says, "and she stayed with us for a week."

The key to going from a family of two to a family of five? Three things help. First, color-coding: Chaucer's clothes are pink, Carter's are green, Tosca's are yellow. Second, a highly organized full-time parent, James. "He's very disciplined," says Jon. "At night, he puts all three down, and no matter what, we don't go in there. When we retreated from that policy, there was hell to pay." Third, help. "I have a family of women," James says—three childcare experts from the same family: one does the day shift during the week, another does dinner and bedtime, the third helps out on weekends.

Despite all that, it's hectic. When the kids were a year old, James' parents were pressed into service as on-site babysitters, and the two men took their first break, a vacation in Las Vegas. "We could not stop talking about the kids," James says. "We couldn't even sleep in for thinking about them."

These days, they try to have evenings out. "Jon plays hockey," says James, "so he gets out." But James rarely does, finding it "difficult to trust someone with my kids, except my parents."

It's a major reason they decided to move back to Texas. With relatives in profusion, "we won't have to rely on just me and Jon," says James. "There are people there we can trust beyond money to take care of the kids. My time will really open up when that happens," he goes on.

And more free time for James is important to both men. As the stay-at-home parent, even with all the help, he had begun to feel, in his words, "like a 1950s housewife"—that is, invisible. When he and Jon were invited to participate in a corporate panel discussion about parenting, the host focused her attention on Jon and suggested that "spouses"—meaning James—"sit this out."

"They were supposed to be talking about parenting," James recalls. "Jon kept telling the host that 'James is really the one who can answer this,' but it made no difference." What was particularly aggravating was that James had gone through hoops of fire to be present at the panel discussion. He had rearranged babysitting schedules, juggled daycare, even taken precious time to get his hair cut and his brows waxed "so I'd look presentable in public." Moreover, when the two men left the apartment, the triplets "began screaming and crying because we were both leaving at once," so add a measure of guilt to the other burdens James had assumed to be able to attend the event. "Then we get there," he says, "and I'm invisible.

"I have a feeling," James goes on, "that as parenting becomes more and more accepted within the gay community, we'll have to overcome this house-spouse issue."

But the children are flourishing. "They have made up their prematurity" in terms of health complications, says Jon. Still, a physical therapist, occupational therapist, and special instruction person work with all three "to help them meet their developmental milestones," as James puts it. So far, "they're a little slow on the milestones, but all are catching up."

The biological connection that James always felt he needed is there, but "everybody has a different theory of who looks like whom," James says. Jon is the parent of record on the birth certificate, with James waiting for the right time to do a second-parent adoption.

Meanwhile, Garcia and Langbert still talk to their surrogate every two or three months. "If we go through surrogacy again," says James, "I would want the same surrogate. I wouldn't want to go through this emotional roller-coaster with someone else; I wouldn't take the chance." They have come a long way from their beginning as people with nothing in common; between the two men and this woman is a singular shared experience that cannot be matched in any other arena of life. As she once carried their children, she'll always carry their best wishes.

Asking the
Right Questions

At the Jewish festival of Passover, four questions are traditionally asked. They are meant to be asked by the children, and the intention is to elicit answers that explain the meaning of the celebration. When partners Paul Fishman and Mike Kurokawa began to observe Passover at the home of their lesbian friends Ellen and Joanne, with no kids present, Joanne routinely added a fifth question. "Ever think about having a kid?" she asked Paul and Mike.

Fishman and Kurokawa had met in 1984 and had been dating for some six months when Fishman first met Ellen. He was starting a psychiatry residency in San Francisco at the time, and Ellen, a "nice Jewish doctor" like himself, was "the kind of woman my parents would have loved me to bring home." The two became friends instead, and two years later, when Ellen began a relationship with Joanne, the couples became acquainted.

They saw each other from time to time over the years—notably, of course, at those Passover seders, when Joanne kept asking the "fifth question." But where the issue of having a child was concerned, both the partners and the couples were out of sync. Parenthood was important to Paul but not so much to Mike, important to Joanne but not equally so to Ellen. Where one person was willing to have some role in some sort of family constellation, his or her partner saw four full-time coparents, all giving equal care. And so the talk of family remained abstract—theoretical—as the seesawing continued between partners and between couples.

Then one day in 1995, at a wonderful Brazilian restaurant in San Francisco, Joanne "popped the question," in Paul Fishman's phrase. It was a fairly simple question: would Paul and Mike have a baby with Joanne and Ellen? Would they create and coparent a child that Joanne would carry and deliver?

That took the theoretical abstraction right out of the equation, confronting Fishman and Kurokawa with what was potentially a radical change in their lives. The very first question, obviously, was whether parenthood was something both wanted.

Mike Kurokawa wasn't sure. "I never expected to be a dad," he says. "I have lots of siblings and nine grown nieces and nephews. I had the uncle thing down. I felt no need to be a parent, nor was there family pressure on me to have a child. So fatherhood didn't figure much in my thinking, which is why I initially didn't know how I would feel going forward. I didn't know if I would be a dad; I just knew I wanted to be there for Paul."

For his part, Paul "didn't want my being a father to get in the way of my relationship with Mike." While he was fixed on the idea of fatherhood, he thought parenthood "necessitated coequal fathers," and Mike simply could not reassure him on that point.

"I had no pattern or model," Mike says. "At the time, I couldn't tell Paul where I would be emotionally. I just didn't know for sure—which was not what Paul wanted to hear." He pauses. "If it were not for Paul, in fact, I would never have done this. Fatherhood wasn't part of my thinking. Life was fine as it was, and it never entered my mind to make such a change."

The irony, Paul says today, "is that Mike is the favorite parent," the one their child always wants to be with. As for Mike, he is grateful that he was pulled reluctantly into what he calls "the opportunity" of fatherhood.

But before he or any of the four putative parents agreed to create a family together, there were a number of issues they needed to thrash out. The four headed up to Sonoma for a marathon weekend of discussion. How would the coparenting work? What would this "family" look like? How would responsibilities be allocated? What about vacations? Whose name or names would the child take? And where the two couples were concerned, was this going to be like marriage or divorce or something else altogether?

"We all four talked about families and about our experiences as children," recalls Mike, as well as about levels of involvement and shared responsibilities. Joanne "wanted our significant involvement," Fishman says. "She wanted the baby to have known fathers. In fact, her idea was for us to be involved up to 50 percent." Joanne also announced that if Fishman and Kurokawa said no to the coparenting with her and Ellen, she was prepared to head for the anonymity of a sperm bank.

The family picture they came up with, Paul says, "was a fifty-fifty deal. The child would spend half the time with Joanne and Ellen and half the time with us. Something like Thanksgiving would be a family holiday with all four parents." As it happens, Paul goes on, the arrangement has evolved into something even more fifty-fifty than originally envisioned, as "we all spend all the holidays together."

They didn't know that at the time, however. At the time, the issue was the agreement to "get pregnant" and the act of doing so.

"Mike and I had a date," Paul says, at a junction in Joanne's cycle that was just right for conception. When Paul's sperm had been collected in a cup, Joanne and Ellen showed up, and all four drove to a fertility clinic where the sperm was implanted in Joanne. They were prepared for nothing to happen, but "the first try did it," says Mike.

It was a four-parent pregnancy. "We went to all the birthing classes together," Mike says. "We told our story everywhere. We were a team." The team was present in the delivery room as well, with Mike, Paul, and Ellen each holding one of Joanne's limbs as she gave birth. And after some minor wrangling, each of the four contributed an element of their son's name: both Paul and Joanne wanted their surnames to "carry on;" Paul and Mike asked for a middle name of Roy in memory of Mike's brother, who had died of AIDS two years earlier; and Ellen proposed the first name. It all came together as Daniel Roy Fishman-Engel, born in September 1996.

Danny went home with his mothers, but on day eight of his life, they brought him to his fathers' house for a *brit,* the Jewish ceremony surrounding the circumcision of a male child. All the grandparents were on hand—three couples and a divorced pair—and it was, says Paul, "an amazingly moving experience." Danny returned to his mothers' house and was there a full month—Joanne was breast-feeding him—but after that month, he started spending one night a week at his fathers'. "How precious this was," Paul recalls, and it grew more precious as Danny spent more time: two nights a week when he reached two months of age, three nights at three months, and so on.

The two sets of parents kept in close touch through all these moves. "We coordinated everything," says Paul. "When Danny moved to a separate bedroom at their house, he did the same at our house. The idea was to keep things consistent." Over the years, the schedule evolved: Danny spends Sunday, Wednesday, and Friday until late Saturday morning with his fathers and the rest of the time with his mothers. It means "we all get

to see him every day," Mike explains, "because one side drops him off at school or whatever, and the other picks him up."

Danny is the son of three doctors and one massage therapist, and both his fathers work out of the house. Paul is a Jungian analyst and psychotherapist, and Mike, the massage therapist, maintains a studio in the house; the patients/clients of the two share a waiting room. Danny has his own room in the house, which is an old Victorian with a small backyard in a cheerful neighborhood. His fathers' house is a mile from his mothers' larger house, also Victorian, but the mothers leave the home to work. Danny attends a prestigious and academically rigorous private day school, which he loves. Deciding to send him there presented his parents with a bit of a dilemma. Danny had been accepted at a number of highly competitive schools, which meant his parents had to make a choice. While his mothers leaned toward the prestigious and academically rigorous choice, his fathers were more comfortable with what Mike describes as a "more soulful, highly diverse school" where the students came from families more on the Mike-Paul socioeconomic level. They talked it through. Joanne and Ellen "acknowledged having some concerns about the issues of diversity and comfort" at their choice of schools, "and they gave us room to work it out." In the end, the men were persuaded by the head of Danny's preschool, who assured them that the resources and discipline of the school preferred by Danny's mothers represented an opportunity not to be missed.

Mostly, the four parents come together around "the nexus," as Mike defines it, that is their son. "The most common way for a kid to have four parents is through divorce and remarriage," says Paul. "Our situation is like divorce without the enmity." Mike bristles a bit at the word "divorce." "It is a coming together," he says, "not a breaking apart. We were two couples that have been drawn closer, not a unit that was sundered."

The schedule is part of it—the chance for all four parents to see their son every day. It is "not without its stress on a kid," says Paul, but "it's what Danny knows, and he's attached to keeping to the schedule." The "shadow problem" with the schedule, as Paul calls it, is that Danny can be "loved too much, showered with too much attention." Mike explains: "When we're with Danny, we interact intensely because we haven't seen him in a day. He constantly gets focused attention from one side or the other because we all schedule our work to have nothing else to do the nights he's with us. That's good developmentally, but it's bad if the kid comes to expect that level of attention. It can be a burden on him." What's more, while Danny had a nanny before he attended preschool, "he has yet to have a baby-sitter," Paul reports; instead he has always been left with grandparents.

For these reasons, the men have "made a conscious effort," Paul says, "to let Danny play by himself in his room and go to sleep by himself"— in short, as Mike puts it, "to leave him alone" for significant portions of time.

Still, they are not convinced that the heavy dose of adult supervision is all that bad for their son. "I grew up in a large extended family in a small town," says Mike. "I dealt with a constellation of adults in parental roles, all telling me what to do and what not to do." Most people have grown up just that way through most of history, he points out. "The ideal of an isolated nuclear family is pretty recent," he claims, "and somewhat foolish."

But Danny's "constellation of adults" doesn't always agree. While the four of them try to talk things through when it comes to their son, there have been bones of contention. Not surprisingly perhaps, the worst of them was money.

The discord surfaced when Danny was 18 months old and Mike had an opportunity to take a severance package and opt out of the corporate environment. He found his way instead to massage therapy, which he loves, and he soon decided to make it his profession and not return to the corporate world at all. Everything about this decision seemed right: Mike was at last doing work he loved, he didn't have to travel, and he certainly didn't miss the corporate scene. The only thing he did miss was the money; as a certified massage therapist with a solid practice, he still earned 60 percent less than he had earned in the corporate environment. It became an issue between the two couples.

Under their original parenting agreement, each parent was to contribute to Danny's upbringing according to his or her ability. But a sudden 60 percent drop in earning ability struck Danny's mothers as a very significant change in the situation. "I had made my career choice for a reason," says Mike. "Among other things, it gave me the flexibility to be more available as a parent." But Danny's mothers "saw me as having chosen not to work."

The perception bothered Paul more than it annoyed Mike. "I know how hard he works and how much it works for him to do this," says Paul. "Together, we earn enough to raise a son if his mothers weren't there." But they were there, with considerably greater earning power than Danny's fathers, which also "confused the issue," at least in Paul's view.

There were "a few very uncomfortable conversations," Mike says, and then, for nearly a year, there was very little conversation at all. "We weren't talking enough," Mike says. "It's a thing no one likes to talk about." Still, the issue "was hanging there," as Paul puts it.

Eventually, he wrote "a long email laying out how we felt, point by point"—Mike helped him "edit out the nonhelpful parts"—and suggesting that all four revisit the issue. "They were open to it," Mike says, and the four agreed to meet in person at Shabbat dinner, the Friday night celebration welcoming the Jewish Sabbath. "After Danny went to bed," Paul recalls, "we stayed up and talked for hours." No one remembers exactly who raised the idea of a minimum contribution in place of a percentage based on income, but everyone seemed to think it a satisfying solution. "We needed to find out what their issue was," Paul says of Joanne and Ellen. "It wasn't the money. It was an issue of fairness." With the idea of a minimum contribution, that issue was squared away, and everyone's emotional needs seemed gratified.

The incident etched in sharp relief the need for regular, open communication. The key to resolving the issue, says Mike, had been "getting it all out in the open" in the first place. And Paul believes that the reason the contention persisted for so long was "because we don't have pillow talk" with Danny's mothers. "Pillow talk" is an essential element of the Fishman-Kurokawa relationship. "Every Sunday night," Paul says, "we spend five minutes at least talking about where we are vis-à-vis one another, Danny, Joanne and Ellen. The idea is that nothing gets carried over, so that even during the week, you know you have Sunday night to clarify and resolve it." It was the lack of intercouple pillow talk that had allowed the issue to fester.

The nearly year-long money issue demonstrated that the couple-to-couple relationship was not perfect. What relationship *is* perfect? Marriage without pillow talk or divorce without enmity, the relationship that Danny's parents have worked out nevertheless works as a structure for four adults and one much-loved boy. He calls them Daddy Paul and Daddy Mike, Mommy Joey and Mommy El—or just by their first names. All five are together at monthly Shabbat dinners, Thanksgiving, and Passover, where each year, all look forward to hearing their son Danny ask the traditional four questions.

Worth the Risk

Most parents are prepared to risk everything for their children. Joe Easton may be prepared to risk his health for his son, Tyler.

Easton is separated from his partner of eight years, Chuck, who is Tyler's other father. By their mutual agreement, in keeping with the terms of a joint custody arrangement, Tyler spends the school year in Calgary, Alberta, with Chuck and Chuck's new partner, while spending vacations with Easton on the coast of Puget Sound in Washington. But when the leaves turn and autumn rolls around, and Tyler must leave the tide pools of the Northwest for the high plains of Alberta, Easton and his son miss each other so much that Joe has been giving serious consideration to uprooting himself and moving to Canada. The catch is that the altitude and pollution of Calgary could be, for this severe asthmatic, quite literally bad for his health.

Yet whatever Easton suffers, whether it's the danger of asthma or the pain of separation, he will still tell you that fatherhood is worth it.

For Joe, the desire to be a father was one of long standing. When he came out in the early 1970s, "there was no legal way to be a gay dad; kids were being taken from gay parents." That changed over the years, and when Joe and Chuck met in 1992, gay parenthood seemed possible.

Their meeting was a natural: Joe worked in the San Francisco Sheriff's Department, and Chuck was a police officer on one of the city's toughest public housing beats. On their second date, they were pressed into service as babysitters for Joe's neighbor on an emergency basis; they spent hours talking about how they both wanted to have children. When in due course they registered as domestic partners at San Francisco's City Hall, they accompanied the event with a commitment ceremony. In front of family and friends, they took letters from the surnames of each and created a new, joint surname, Easton. It signified "a new beginning for the two of us," Joe Easton says, "a way of saying that this was our new family." They had even picked out a name for their first child: Tyler Easton.

For two and a half years, they tried to impregnate a surrogate, but after what Easton describes as "no minor effort," the woman proved infertile. They next tried an adoption fair, where Joe had no qualms about being blunt. "I'm a gay man," he told the agencies lined up at the fair. "I have a lover. Will you deal with us without robbing us?" Most were not willing, but an adoption facilitator named Nancy Hurwitz Kors was. "We went in and met with her on a Tuesday morning," Joe recalls. Their "requirements" were minimal; they placed no restrictions on the gender

or race of the child, but they were adamant that the birthmother be clean and sober. As members of law enforcement, both men had had experience with babies born addicted. Since they felt that having two gay dads would be a burden for any child, they didn't want to add to the burden the problems that might derive from a drug-using mother. Kors advised them it would take one to two years to find a clean birthmother. They resigned themselves to a long wait and went home. When Kors called back later that day to say that she had found them a perfect match, they were as stunned as they were thrilled.

The baby was due in May. They met the birthmother in March and liked her very much. She liked them as well, choosing them over 12 other families to be the parents of her baby. She was Filipino, poor, unable to care for a child, and eager for her baby to be born a U.S. citizen. She was impressed with Joe and Chuck—their stability, their attitudes on raising a child, and the fact that they were law enforcement officers. She believed they would take good care of her child. In their turn, they assured her the adoption could be as open as she chose, that "she could make the baby as big or little a part of her life as she wanted," and that even if she closed the connection with her child, she could open it at any time.

Tyler arrived earlier than expected, but since he was full-term, it was likely the birthmother had miscalculated her date of conception. It was mid-April when she went into labor—a surprise for everyone involved. Joe and Chuck headed down the highway to San Jose, only to find that the birth was "close" but not that close. "The birthmother and I walked up and down for six hours to make the baby come," Joe recalls. She talked about how difficult life was in the Philippines; Joe talked about his work, his and Chuck's efforts to have a baby, and his plans to be a full-time father. The conversation "made her all the more determined" to place her child with them, he says, and the walking must have done the trick, because by the end of it, Tyler was ready to emerge.

The two fathers-to-be helped in the delivery, each one holding one of the birthmother's legs, both assisting with her breathing. "That was the best," Joe says simply. It was six days before his fiftieth birthday.

The birthmother at first chose not to hold the baby; she was even housed in a separate ward where she "would not feel guilty about not nursing." When postpartum depression set in, Joe was there to hold her hand, and he was there when she said goodbye to her son. She entered the nursery, held the baby, and "had some time with him," Joe says. Then she left.

Finalizing the adoption of Tyler was by no means smooth and by no means pleasant. "Being approved to be a father," says Joe, "was tougher and took more paperwork than getting into law enforcement." The home inspections felt intrusive, as they were questioned at length and their lives pointedly scrutinized.

Then the social worker demanded they attend classes in how to take care of babies—this despite the fact that Joe was a paramedic, had run a well-baby clinic for two years in the navy, had operated an emergency room on a navy base, and had obtained Red Cross recertification a month before Tyler was born. What's more, both Joe and Chuck had younger siblings whose diapers they had changed regularly and with whose crying jags they were well acquainted.

Worst of all, the social worker's interviewing style quickly demonstrated that her motives were dubious at best, malicious at worst, as her questions ranged from the insulting to the surreal. Joe Easton remembers the tenor of those questions: "When do you plan to have sex with your child? Will you take pictures and sell them? Have you ever known a child molester, and how important is that person in your life?" The Eastons were staggered; the questions were patently illegal. "Answer or you'll lose your child," the social worker told them. The two men turned the issue over to their lawyer, and the head of a national gay lawyers group wrote a blistering letter to the social worker's agency. The social worker backed off and the questions were withdrawn, but the incident made the whole adoption process take longer and cost more. And the social worker was "not even reprimanded" for her actions, Joe Easton says—a fact that rankles to this day.

Becoming Tyler's fathers, says Joe, "was the best thing that happened" to the Eastons, the fulfillment of a long-sought dream. That same year, however, saw Joe's health deteriorate markedly. He was by now a severe asthmatic, suffering daily attacks from California's bad air quality and operating on low energy. The Easton family moved to Petaluma in April 1998, when Tyler was about a year old, but that did not ameliorate the situation, and in 1999, Deputy Sheriff Joe Easton applied for and was granted disability retirement from the sheriff's office. He took on a new profession—that of full-time father.

When Tyler was not quite two, Joe and Chuck heard through their adoption facilitator that their son's birthmother was back in the United States. They took Tyler to visit her. Chuck, according to Joe, was "more nervous than if he had been going up against gun-wielding bad guys," worrying about what grade the birthmother would give them as parents.

He needn't have worried. She found her son healthy, happy, and well-mannered and was "very happy he was with us," Joe says. But she would not divulge her address in the Philippines, and there has been no contact with her since that time.

In the meantime, relations between Joe and Chuck were withering. In 2000, as happens in half of all marriages in America, their union broke apart. "We drove to the divorce lawyer in separate cars," Joe recalls. "We knew we didn't want to go to court over custody." These are two men who had served long careers in law enforcement; they had seen plenty of domestic discord and its effect on children—enough to know they did not want their child to be similarly affected. They determined on joint custody; it means both have to decide any issues related to Tyler.

"It hasn't been easy separating," says Joe. "We have both almost bitten our tongues off time and again. But we realized early on that the only thing that would help Tyler was for us to remain civil, that if either of us puts the other down, it would get back to him. He is the reason we remain civil."

Both men were careful to move to places with good schools. Chuck headed for Calgary with a new partner and began a new life, even applying for Canadian citizenship. Joe moved to a small town in Washington where the air quality is good enough that his condition has improved measurably. He also sought a location with a racial mix and a large enough Filipino population for Tyler to feel at home.

Tyler has always known he is adopted, and he knows he has two dads. When he has asked why his household doesn't include a mommy, Joe has told him that "I'm a daddy who likes other men." In both his homes, Tyler has friends who have gay parents, too, so although he knows most children have a mother and father, he also knows that not all children do. He asks occasionally about his own mother and wonders if she could come and live with them all. "She would be welcome," Joe tells him, "but as a friend."

In Washington, Tyler and Joe spend time exploring tide pools, identifying crabs and shellfish, watching the Discovery Channel, and making quilts. "He does the cutting, and I do the sewing," says Joe, a passionate quilt maker. Tyler also loves all kinds of emergency vehicles and wants to drive them all when he grows up. "When he was two, he was better at working the inside of a police car than most recruits," says his doting father. He satisfies his driving yearnings now by riding his miniature "hog" around the neighborhood. Tyler also wants to be a paleontologist when he grows up and has memorized the name of every dinosaur that ever roamed the earth. Joe loves to take him places—like to the Monterey Aquarium—but also just "to sit with him, reading and doing projects."

It was Tyler's choice to go to school in Calgary. It doesn't rain as much there, which gives him more opportunity to play outside, and there is more going on there to dazzle a little boy—the zoo, primarily, but also hockey and basketball teams, museums and cultural institutions. But there is also something missing in Calgary—his father, Joe, and the reality of their separation is as hard for Tyler as it is for Joe.

For Joe, Tyler's departure can be thunderous in its suddenness—one day his presence fills the house; the next day he's gone. It creates a great hole in Joe's life, which begins to feel isolated and isolating. The community is small and tends to be conservative, although all Joe's neighbors know he is gay "and there are no problems with that," he says. He has a list of projects he wants to accomplish before Tyler comes back for vacation, he cooks for the monthly dinner and bingo at the county's gay organization, he volunteers for the quilt guild, and he busies himself making soft sculptures, quilts, and leather clothing, a hobby/job from long ago he has taken up again in retirement. But it is hard to fill the days.

Dating is not particularly easy, either. When Tyler is there, says Joe, "I don't go out." Even with Tyler away, Joe is still "a single dad, and a lot of men walk when they hear there's a child in the picture."

Tyler, of course, wants his fathers together. His ongoing fantasy is that everybody will live on the same block so that he can walk from house to house. Joe worries about the pollution in Calgary. He wants to live "to see Tyler graduate and give me grandchildren," and for that, he needs to take care of his health. But making do with a daily phone call and a trip to Calgary every six weeks or so, as finances allow, has been very, very hard. "I have got to get used to it," he says; "otherwise, it'll ruin my life." Get used to it or get on the road: it's a tough choice.

Tyler's bedtime prayer asks God to "bless my daddies Joe, Chuck, and Rob." It's been hard for Joe to accept that Tyler now calls Chuck's partner "Daddy" as well. But in the end, being Tyler's father is the best part of Joe's life. "I walked away from a lot of things to have this life with Tyler," he says, "and it is every bit worth it."

It may even be worth risking his health.

Open to the
Possibilities

A telemarketer phoning the Dyar-Place home one evening reached Naya Dyar-Place, three and a half years of age at the time. "May I speak to your mommy?" the telemarketer asked. "No," said Naya, "I have two dads."

The two, Tim and Dan Dyar-Place, hope that Naya and her brother, Cameron, feel special for having two dads. At the same time, they try to expose their children to all sorts of family configurations—children with mothers and fathers, with two mothers, two fathers, one father, one mother—so they can "see the world as consisting of lots of different options," in Dan's phrase, and so they'll know that "families are people who love each other." They certainly know it about their own family.

It was a family that took some time to come into being. Tim and Dan first became a couple in 1983. Both had always wanted to become fathers, and both had always assumed it wasn't possible. "For me," says Dan, "my greatest disappointment when I came out was that in my mind, it meant not being a dad. I was twenty-two, and it was crushing."

To compensate, says Tim, "we would play with other people's kids, and we would talk about being fathers. But it was so foreign and far away. This was the early eighties. We put it out of minds. We were busy getting our careers together and buying a car and a house."

But it was never far out of their minds. By the early nineties, they were ready to enroll in a class for California's fost-adopt program, which licenses people to be foster parents with the intention to adopt. Everyone in the class in which they enrolled was gay or lesbian, and everyone except Tim and Dan eventually got children through the program. For the Dyar-Places, life at this time took a different direction: they had just finished the fost-adopt class when Dan, a human resources manager for J. C. Penney, was transferred to Dallas. Although openly gay, Dan did not think to mention to his employer that a partner would be moving with him, so the company handled Dan's relocation, while Tim had to pay his own way. Times have changed since then, as the Dyar-Places' experience would show.

Once they arrived in Texas, Dyar and Place picked right up where they had left off in California, in a dual licensing process for foster parenting and adoption. They would later learn that they were the first openly gay couple to take the class; in fact, says Dan, they were evidently "the talk of Child Protective Services." All they knew at the time, however, was that nobody was placing any babies with them. Finally a social worker suggested they would have a better chance "if there's a stay-at-

home parent." So Tim quit his job as a real estate appraiser to take on the full-time profession of being a parent to foster children.

They fostered nine children over three years. The children ranged in age from infancy to six years old. Because Tim had studied nursing and had worked as a nurse technician, he and Dan tended to be given foster babies with health problems and special needs—often a result of their mothers having used drugs. The two would lavish love and attention on these children—on all the children—investing themselves and their emotions heavily, hoping and praying to adopt each one of them, only to have all of the children returned to their biological families. It was agonizing.

The Dyar-Places' attempts to adopt a child eventually prompted a friend to offer them a surrogate pregnancy. It was something the men had never even considered. "Having a biological child was not an issue for either of us," says Tim, but suddenly surrogacy with this friend—call her Ilana—seemed a solution. Ilana, who is black—Tim and Dan are both white—had a child of her own and had enjoyed an easy pregnancy. Realizing the kind of commitment surrogacy could mean, however, they all went to counseling together. "We wanted to make sure it was something the three of us could do," Tim says. Then they began the process of insemination.

It was a do-it-yourself operation. Ilana used an ovulation kit bought in the local pharmacy to monitor her cycle, and each month, at her fertile time, Tim and Dan would mix their sperm into, fittingly, a baby food jar. Ilana would then lie in bed, insert the sperm, and go to sleep. In the ninth month of trying, with the home pregnancy test coming up negative nine times out of nine, Ilana announced that they would need to set a cutoff date. They agreed to a total of 12 inseminations—three more. On the next try, the test again came up negative, but this time Ilana was puzzled; she really thought she was pregnant. She tried the test again two days later: positive. She was pregnant, and Dan and Tim were ecstatic.

Although she had been a veritable "birthing machine" when she carried and delivered her other child, Ilana's pregnancy this time was no picnic. She was sick for much of it, so for her last trimester, she and her three-year-old moved in with Tim and Dan. There were no other foster children in the Dyar-Place household at the time, so Tim took care of Ilana's child and ministered to Ilana's needs as well. It was November 1998, five weeks to the due date, and everything seemed to be coming together at last. Then the phone rang, and the picture changed.

The call was from a social worker the Dyar-Places had worked with in the past. A newborn had just been added to his caseload, the child of a mother from whom four children had previously been removed. It was an African-American boy born prematurely and addicted to cocaine. He was in the neonatal intensive care unit, on a heart monitor, and with the rigid muscle tone that is typical of crack babies. "He is your best shot at adoption," the social worker told Tim and Dan.

They went for a walk to talk it over. "The surrogate is in our house, five weeks from delivery," Dan recalls their summarizing of the situation. "Under Texas law, she could take the baby at birth if she decided to." By the same token, they had had "five foster children that year, all of whom had gone back," and here was their first real chance to adopt a child, the goal they had been aiming toward for more than three years.

In a way, everything was suddenly possible, but nothing was for sure. At best, after years of fighting to become fathers, they might suddenly become the parents of two children at once. But could they handle two—especially if one was a sick newborn with considerable special needs, a child who conceivably might not recover? Tim answered for them both: "What if this is the child God wants us to have? What if this is our child and we say no?" Of course, they said yes.

Their son Cameron, the older child, was the first to arrive in their house. Three and a half pounds at birth, he spent 10 days in the NICU; Tim went every day to feed him. Their daughter, Naya, was born five weeks later—at home, under the supervision of a midwife; she weighed seven and a half pounds at the time, although she is now not quite as big as her brother.

"Two newborns were more work than I thought," says Tim. Fortunately, Ilana was there to take care of Cameron while Tim attended to Naya; it helped Ilana do some nurturing while keeping her distance from

Naya, something she herself was adamant about. After two weeks, Ilana moved out; her involvement in Naya's life now is minimal. Dan and Tim hope she will be a friend and confidant to their daughter, and they expect that Naya may develop a relationship with Ilana's daughter, but they acknowledge that "this may work out other than we have scripted it."

Cameron's health problems occupied significant time and energy. He needed massage therapy to build "down" the overtoned muscle, was sensitive to light, had tongue thrust—which would make speech difficult—and there were medical experts who thought he would never walk without surgery. The state provided an early childhood intervention specialist who came to the home, coordinated a range of therapies—

massage, speech, physical, and occupational—and trained Tim as well; for the first two and a half years of Cameron's life, the specialist was there once a week. In addition, Tim worked with his son every day, and in time, the work had its effect. As for the surgeries to help Cameron walk, none were needed to create a "very rambunctious" little boy who walks only when he can't run.

Raising a child also had the effect of exploding a couple of myths that had held Dyar and Place in thrall. One myth was that the biological child is easier to raise. Nonsense, says Tim. "Cameron was the easiest kid in the world, and Naya can be a major diva." Another myth, one that Dan worried about, was that "it wasn't possible to love your kids the same. But you know what? I do. I love different things about them because they're different people, but I love them equally." Nor is there any distinction, in the children or in their fathers' affection, between biological child and adoptee.

In fact, "we really don't know who Naya's biological father is," says Tim. "She doesn't seem to look like one or the other of us," although both sets of grandparents are convinced she is biologically their side of the family. The children themselves are best friends—rarely apart—and their parents think the fact that they are different sexes makes their relationship easier and less competitive. Dan, who was convinced he would be a "parent who wasn't going to impose any gender stereotypes," is amused at how naturally his son and daughter fall into them. In a roomful of toys left over from their foster-parenting days, a tiny Naya instantly reaches for the dolls, while Cameron picks up a doll only to shove it into his truck and push it down the stairs.

The children lived only a short time in their native state. "Texas was very good to us," Tim says. "It gave us our family"—and to some extent helped support the family. They are particularly grateful to the gay and lesbian Cathedral of Hope in Dallas and to the entire gay community there. In fact, the men maintained "a large gay connection" in Texas, perhaps because to be openly gay in Texas requires the support of other gays.

But there was another side to their life in Dallas. The two men found the city, with its large black and Latino populations, a self-segregating place—and thus perhaps not the best environment for two white men with an African-American and a mixed-race child. There was the time they took the kids to Playland and a nice-looking older woman asked them: "Who do these little niglets belong to?" "They belong to me," Tim answered. At other times, he heard his children referred to as "cute little pickaninnies" and as "little niggers."

There was more. Their neighborhood was made up mostly of families with high-school age children, leaving Dan and Tim, with their toddlers, feeling slightly isolated. The isolation went beyond not being invited to the block party. One Halloween, someone scrawled "Fags" on the house in shaving cream, and eggs were thrown at their front door. On a nearby bridge, within view of their house, another huge "Fags out!" had been spray-painted. The police suspected the teenagers across the street, and while there were no verbal assaults nor any physical menacing, it was not pleasant having that "looming over you," says Dan.

Add in the fact that both men wanted their children to grow up closer to their grandparents, and it seemed ample motivation to go back to California. In 2001, Dan was able to arrange a reverse transfer, and nine years after his "solo" move from California to Texas, J. C. Penney paid for the relocation of his entire family the other way.

Back in southern California, things are different. Where their kids had few friends nearby in Texas, their house has now become the neighborhood hangout. Where they were not invited to the block party in Dallas, the 2002 block party was held at their house. Dan's parents are 35 minutes away, Tim's 20 minutes away, and the kids spend a lot of time with both.

Tim finds it easier to be a stay-at-home dad in California and finds that he has "more in common with the stay-at-home moms in the neighborhood than with other gay people"—although he sometimes feels like the neighborhood therapist, which can be burdensome. His pet peeve is those parents, gay or straight, who hire a nanny for their children while they go to work. "My kids do something amazing every day," he says, "and I don't have to miss it. When people tell me how lucky I am to stay at home, it irritates me because it's not a question of luck; we've made it happen. They tell me I'm lucky, then drive off in their BMW while I get into my Dodge Dart." Adds Dan: "We used to have the biggest house, and we downsized twice to make it possible for Tim to stay at home. It's our choice, not luck. And it's not as if we feel we're doing without, either."

If they're doing without anything, it's sleep. When they finally decided to leave the kids with the grandparents and take a vacation with friends in an art community in Arkansas, the friends wanted to party, and they just wanted to sleep—although it was nice to have some adult conversation for a change.

They are members of the Pop Luck Club, the huge, Los Angeles–based gay fathers organization, and they're happy to brave the freeways to a Pop Luck event so their kids can see other families like themselves.

They are perhaps surprised to find themselves a family, were caught unawares by the way their family came into being and by what it looks like. That may make it all the more precious.

"Your child is out there," says Tim Dyar-Place—even if he or she is not the child you expected and shows up when you're not sure you're ready. "You have in your mind the child you want," he goes on, "and the child that comes your way may be entirely different—may look different or be a different age from what you think. You just don't know. But open your heart and your mind; be open to what the universe brings you: it's your child."

The Network

"If you want something done, ask a hairdresser," quips Ron Preston, hairdresser par excellence. After all, talk about networking! Who has a better set of connections than a beauty salon owner into whose hands the town's women place their looks and their trust—women ranging from business entrepreneurs to the wives of the town's prominent burghers to working mothers, the volunteer squad, even the garden club mafia?

Ron Preston owns and operates the top hair salon in Wichita Falls, Texas, and the network that is his clientele sprang into action when Ron and his partner, Greg Thomas, were adopting their daughter, Samantha. It seemed that every time a need arose, it was satisfied via a hairdressing connection. To the deeply religious Preston, this wasn't coincidence; it was "divine intervention," God working His will through the means at hand.

In fact, divine intervention was at work bringing Samantha home to her fathers from the very beginning—literally as well as figuratively—for it was through their pastor at the Wichita Falls Metropolitan Community Church that Preston and Thomas learned about the pregnant birthmother who was prepared to place her child for adoption. The two men had met in 1994 and held their holy union ceremony at the church in 1995. The issue of children was always in their thoughts.

But of course, both thought the issue must remain only a thought. Ron Preston, who had always loved kids, began praying to become an uncle the moment his brother married—without ever considering parenthood as a possibility. The possibility was, if anything, even more remote after he and Greg became a couple—two men living openly as partners in a small town in Texas. That alone made parenthood seem unlikely, if not out of the question. Preston also wasn't sure how his parents might react to his adopting a child; Greg, whose parents "have never been accepting of my relationship with Ron," was pretty certain his family would not react well at all. And, says Ron, the two men simply "didn't know it would be as easy as it was."

But in the late 1990s, Ron began praying over the possibility of becoming a father, and he began discussing the issue with the pastor of the largely gay and lesbian congregation at Metropolitan Community Church. A few months later, the pastor called Ron and Greg. The birthmother of two children who had been adopted by another family in the church was pregnant again, and the adoptive family felt unable to take this third child. Ron and Greg should also know, the pastor said, that the child would almost surely be biracial and might conceivably be born with

health problems resulting from the birthmother's behavior. Would they consider adopting the child?

There it was. Right before them. In their faces, so to speak. The very thing Ron had been praying over, the very eventuality the two of them had been talking about for months, if not years. They knew the other family in the church, knew their adopted children and found them "wonderful . . . perfect . . . absolutely beautiful and very sweet." The medical records on the birthmother, who was incarcerated at the time of her pregnancy, were clean. Through five months of regular visits, they also learned something of the birthmother's history—that she herself had suffered abuse as a child, and that she had placed her other children for adoption rather than take a chance on repeating the cycle of neglect and maltreatment. "Clearly," says Greg, "she was smart enough to know that her kids should not be with her."

It seemed to the two men that for all her troubles and the sorrows of her life, the birthmother had the best interests of her children at heart, and that in giving them to others to raise she was making the ultimate sacrifice and demonstrating the greatest kind of love. There was a kind of nobility about it.

And they already knew they wanted this baby. Ron's take on it was that "natural parents don't have a choice. If this child is born with problems, it's because God has meant it that way and because He knows we can handle it." Still, they wanted to meet the birthmother, and she wanted to meet them. They found a woman concerned that her baby would be well cared for and that she would have what she needed to deliver a healthy baby. Preston and Thomas assured her of both, undertaking the financial responsibility of maintaining her throughout the rest of her pregnancy.

It was quite a pregnancy. Ron found himself craving foods he normally finds impossible to swallow, much less digest: jalapeño peppers, enchiladas, hot salsa—the very foods, it turns out, that the birthmother was craving. He found the pregnancy "the most wonderful thing I never want to experience personally." Ditto for Greg; observing the pregnancy—and the birth—made him "happy not to be a woman."

They were not supposed to observe the birth; prison regulations forbade anyone in the delivery room but the mother and medical personnel. In fact, Greg and Ron weren't even supposed to know that the birthmother had gone into labor, but by prearranged code, they got the phone call at 7:30 on a Friday evening. Ron instantly headed for the hospital and sashayed "right past the guard on her room as if I was going somewhere else." He headed for the nurses' station, and that's where the hair salon network kicked in. The nurse on duty just happened to be a client of

Ron's. She made a call to the Preston-Thomas lawyer, and he arranged for Ron and Greg to enter the birthing room.

"We didn't know what to anticipate," says Ron. "We had had no physical contact with the birthmother before this except through a plate glass window and via a telephone intercom." Now they were with her at her most intimate and most vulnerable. The men "touched her belly," Greg recalls, "the sort of thing moms and dads do as a matter of course." While Greg went home at around 3:30 A.M. to get some fresh clothing and catch a nap, Ron stayed at the birthmother's side. In fact, he was her only support person throughout her labor and delivery; the two of them "talked the whole time, and I tried to make sure she was comfortable." Ron did not sleep—"not one wink," he says—from the time labor began on Friday evening till 7:19 the next morning. Greg was back by then, so they were both in the room holding on to the birth 1mother for dear life when their daughter was born. "It was a miracle," says Greg.

Ron called his parents at once. "Granddad?" he said when his father picked up the phone. "Your granddaughter is here." His folks came immediately, as did friends, for a joyous birth celebration. Greg, whose parents are devout members of the Church of Christ, had not yet told them that he and Ron were planning to adopt. When he called the day Samantha was born and announced that there was "a new baby," his mother asked if it was a puppy. "No," Greg replied, "a little girl." "What's she going to do without a mommy?" "Be loved by two daddies," came the reply.

The two daddies spent the night of Samantha's first day in the hospital's Almost Home Room, a special setup for adoptive parents and their babies. The nurses, doctors, and all the hospital personnel were wonderful to them; there were "no second glances," says Greg. Ron, who had now gone for 48 hours without sleep, "just crashed" and had to be awakened by a nurse when he missed the alarm for Samantha's feeding. In fact, Samantha never woke up for her feeding, either, which terrified her fathers at first. "From day one, she would sleep through the night," says Greg.

The plan was for Ron to adopt first as a single parent in a process that was supposed to take six months. But the Preston-Thomas lawyer lived next door to a judge who was willing to expedite the process. Of course, it may not be entirely coincidental that the lawyer's wife was a client of Ron's, a fact that may have made its way from neighbor to neighbor. What is certainly a fact is that the judge signed off on everything having to do with the adoption just before going on vacation, so what should have taken six months took only three, and Ron became Samantha's legal

parent—inscribed as such on her birth certificate. The individual who wrote up the birth certificate, by the way, was another Ron client. The network indeed seemed to be everywhere.

But Ron saw something else at work. Shortly after the adoption was finalized, the judge who had expedited the process died. For Ron, this was "too much"—too much coincidence, too much of a near miss, too much favor bestowed on his family. He saw "God's hand in it." He had prayed for that expedited adoption, he says, and "the way everything fell into place was amazing."

Everything fell into place at home as well. Well, almost everything. Samantha was colicky and prone to infections till she was diagnosed as lactose intolerant; once her fathers changed her formula, she became an angel. And something of a princess as well. "She's so bossy she'll probably grow up to be a CEO," says Greg. And Ron says that while "the best part is watching her discover something, the hardest is teaching her that there are boundaries." It's an ongoing course of instruction, as Samantha tests the parameters of her world and the will of her fathers. Greg recalls the time she had one leg up on the coffee table. "Put that foot on the ground," Ron told her. She obeyed—and simultaneously put her other foot up on the table. Admits her father: "It's hard to stay on top of those boundaries that keep her safe."

Keeping Samantha safe is everything to her fathers. When they rock her to sleep at night, they sometimes find themselves just gazing at her, wordlessly, for long minutes, half an hour, even an hour at a time.

It is perhaps because Samantha is so precious to them that Greg finds his family's attitude so painful. When one of Ron's clients—the network again!—threw a baby shower for Samantha and some 60 people showed up, Greg's mother refused to come. "It's not the racial issue," he maintains;

"it's because two men are raising a baby." On the credenza in his parents' house that is covered with family photos, there is none of Samantha. Greg believes it is "so that my mother doesn't have to explain that her son is gay and raising a child."

Even in the pain, however, there is room for hope. While his mother wouldn't come to the shower, his father did. It was highly emotional for Greg to realize that his father was "taking a stand" in support of him. Ron believes that Greg's parents "bend in the way they can. They never forget Samantha's birthday, and they send Christmas gifts to all three of us." But whatever the estrangement, Greg is adamant that "I'm going to live my life as I want to."

If some parental support is lacking, more surprising is what the two men see as a dearth of support from the gay community. They are quite sure they are the first adoptive gay fathers in town—there are a number of adoptive lesbian mothers—but their closeness to old gay friends has worn thin. In fact, says Greg, of their "old crowd of eight to ten people" they once saw regularly, they remain close only to Samantha's godfather and his partner. Partly, they believe, the fall-off is because "we rejected so many invitations so we could stay at home with Samantha. We can't go out at eight at night anymore."

But partly, they also blame what Ron calls "immaturity in the gay community." While he grants that "the smaller the town, the harder it is for gays to be a cohesive group," he also has found "a lot of competition and not a lot of support" among the gay community in his town. Greg's feeling is that "other gay men don't understand" the desire to have children, and in their failure to understand, oppose the idea of gay men becoming fathers.

Preston and Thomas want more people to know that gay men can indeed become fathers, and that they can, in Ron's words, "do as good a job as women." They are certain that their daughter lacks for nothing in terms of love, devotion, discipline, and caring. And while they are coequal caregivers, each has assumed a slightly different parental function. "I've taken on the nurturing role," says Ron; he bathes her, feeds her, and takes her to daycare, and he is also the "stickler for strict routine," in Greg's phrase. Greg does the heavy lifting of childcare—it was he who washed the dirty diapers back in Samantha's diaper days—and is typically the one Samantha calls when she is trying to get away with not going to sleep.

But Preston and Thomas in no way feel isolated as gay dads. "I don't feel like a 'gay' father," says Ron, drawing quote marks with his intonation. "I don't feel people looking at us. We have found a very accepting environment." The people with whom they interact these days are couples, mostly straight couples who have children with whom their daughter can play. They feel strong support from friends without children as well, from Ron's parents—who are, in Ron's word, "besotted" by their granddaughter—and of course from Ron's clientele, that network of beautifully coiffed, perfectly manicured women a hairdresser knows he can count on.

Dream On

Shortly before his companion of 20 years died of AIDS, Kevin Brown had a dream about a little boy with dark hair, dark eyes, two thin arms, and one crippled leg. He was filled with love for this little boy, and in the dream, he turned to a man he and his partner knew as a casual acquaintance and asked: "Can we keep him?" Brown awakened from the dream in tears. He interpreted it as a lesson he had learned from his partner's heroic dying, and he told his partner as much: "Because of you, John, I can look at this little boy as a child and not as damaged goods." Both men agreed that the presence of the acquaintance in the dream, a man named Craig George, was meaningful. "Craig is someone who doesn't look at me as a sick individual," said John. Two days later, John died.

Many months later, Kevin Brown and Craig George had become a couple. They had decided to adopt a child, and they were exploring the idea of international adoption with a social worker who had connections to Bulgarian orphanages. The men considered that they were still in the earliest stages of investigation and inquiry, so when the social worker began to tell them about available orphans, they listened politely, even though they believed that "choosing" a specific child was months away.

She scrolled down the list. "Here is a little boy who is a year old," the social worker said; "he'll be two by the time you can adopt. And by the way, there's something wrong with one of his legs." Kevin Brown did a mental double-take; if he had been half-listening a moment before, he was now all ears as the social worker went on. "He was born with his feet turned in," she said. "It's not uncommon. In the United States, doctors would fit a brace to reshape the muscles." That's when Craig turned to Kevin and said: "Did I ever tell you that I was born with feet turned in and had to wear a brace as a child?"

"That's our son," said Kevin Brown.

It would take another nine months before Kevin's pronouncement came true completely, but then, it had taken a long time to get to the moment of recognition—that instant awareness of his dream as prophecy.

For Kevin, it had all begun many years before—with his fervent desire to have a child. It was a desire he had put aside and put on hold as John's illness held the couple in thrall for nine full years. By the time Kevin and Craig had come together, Kevin felt his biological clock ticking; both men wanted children, and both agreed to start a family sooner rather than later. They hadn't really known where to begin, however, until a neighbor across the street put them in touch with that social worker who specialized in adoptions.

The social worker told them about a range of options. "With a biological child," says Craig George, "the only decision is yes or no—to have the child or not. But with adoption, there are lots of decisions to make." They thought about mixed-race and special-needs children, "but we decided we didn't feel fully equipped for either of those options," George says. "It was enough for us to adopt." Besides, adds Kevin, "there seemed plenty of prospective parents in the United States, where most babies are adopted. Most foreign orphans are not adopted, so on balance, it seemed a better idea—and a better way to match the need to do something good and our personal needs." There was another factor as well: the fear that with domestic adoption, there could conceivably "be an issue later on," a knock on the door years after the fact by a biological relative. For Brown and George, international adoption seemed the right choice.

But "international adoption" is a broad category, within which options and limitations vary, country to country. Only some countries allow a single man to adopt—and since almost none allow gay couples to adopt, the two had decided that Kevin would be the father-of-record internationally, and they would readopt together in the United States. Some of the countries that do allow a single man to adopt only allow him to adopt boys; some only allow girls. In some countries, there are age requirements. And so on and so forth—a patchwork of rules, regulations, and requirements that seem to change routinely. The social worker helped them sort through the jumble and winnow down the list to not quite half a dozen countries in which they might legally adopt.

One of the countries was Bulgaria, and as it happened the social worker knew a New York–based adoption lawyer, Bulgarian born, who had once served as a judge on the Bulgarian bench. It meant that on that day when the social worker started going down the list of available orphans, the day that Kevin experienced the shock of recognition over the little boy who had "something wrong with one of his legs," there would be legal expertise and legal support available to help them make him their son.

Medical expertise and support were also available. Craig George's sister is a pediatric emergency room nurse. She flew to Bulgaria with them to observe not just the leg, which doctors had already told them was "nothing to worry about," but Nikolas's overall health. Craig, for one, was worried about attachment disorder. In his mind's eye, he envisioned an ill-equipped, understaffed orphanage in a declining nation. He saw caregivers unable to give sufficient attention to all the children needing to bond. He feared the physiological, emotional, cognitive, and social consequences to the baby boy he and Kevin already saw as their son.

On the day the men arrived to meet Nikolas, he had been taken to the hospital for physical therapy; that was the remedy applied for his leg in the absence of the corrective brace Craig had worn as a child. It had worked. The physical therapy had basically corrected the problem, although Nikolas retained some psychological scars from the pain he suffered as the therapy was applied and injections given.

That may be why Kevin's and Craig's first view of their son was of a sneering little boy brought out of the hospital by nurses on a fine spring day. "He looked at us like that because it was men who always gave him the shots," Craig explains. The sneer lasted 15 seconds, and then Niko-

las began laughing and playing happily with the two men. "They let us play with him for a couple of hours," Kevin recalls, and in that short time, the three of them bonded as a family.

"That," says Craig, in an assertive rejoinder to his original worry, "is a mark of the very good care in Bulgarian orphanages." Both men speak almost reverentially of their experience in Bulgaria. "This was once a highly successful country with few orphanages," says Kevin, "and it is only since the fall of the Soviet Union that the orphanages began to fill up. But they don't necessarily applaud the idea of foreign adoptions, and they are very careful about them."

Careful indeed. When Brown and George heard the process would take "months," they assumed, like the New Yorkers they are, that that meant maybe three months. It didn't, and nothing the men did could expedite the process. "We had to wait on line like everybody else," Kevin says.

The combination of Bulgarian caution and American bureaucracy ensured that it would be almost a year before they could bring Nikolas to the States. "We had been forewarned to notarize every piece of paper because it then has to go to the county clerk to certify that it's notarized, then to the New York department of state to certify that New York is a county, then to the U.S. state department to certify that New York is a state—for every piece of paper," Kevin laments. Some of the required pieces of paper, moreover, seemed ludicrous. One demand, for example, was for a statement that Kevin had never been institutionalized. Another was for proof that he was never married. "How do I prove negatives?" he asked the lawyer. He managed to prove both with letters from appropriate authorities, but of course both had to be notarized and certified. Then one was sent back because it lacked his middle initial.

Eventually, however, the process worked. Nikolas was legally adopted by Kevin under Bulgarian law, and he was granted a visa to the United States. He moved from a Bulgarian orphanage to the East Side of Manhattan. "We had made all sorts of promises to ourselves about our parenting," says Kevin—"no television, no help, no bribes. We broke all of them."

"It was such a life change for us in every way," Kevin recalls. "We even had to be so much more efficient at work." Craig became the stay-at-home dad—more or less. He worked from home with the help of a part-time nanny and part-time office aide. What they did *not* want for their child was what they saw around them: a lot of two-profession households in which the children were "turned over to a stranger or to television." So they "made a conscious decision not to have a live-in housekeeper/nanny who would make it too easy." Together, they managed.

Nikolas had been born with another name entirely. It was not only difficult for Americans to pronounce, it also translated into English as "prison." They changed his name to that of one of Bulgaria's patron saints, with the middle name of George, after Craig's family, and the last name of Brown. They have kept the Bulgarian spelling to maintain their son's link with his native land and so that "he will always have to explain why it's spelled that way," says Craig.

Nikolas, who is "a caring, giving child," according to both fathers, had no separation issues and adjusted quickly, although for the first year, he still could not bear to have his leg touched. "He would scream when we tried to clip his toenails," Kevin says. He had been with them about six months when they knew they wanted another child. "We wanted to make a family instead of just being two guys with a son," says Craig. "And we also did it for Nikolas. In case he ever felt alone in the world, here would be someone from his country of origin."

They alerted their lawyer and asked him to be on the lookout for a child about 18 months younger than Nikolas. The lawyer found him, and Kevin went over to Bulgaria to meet Alex, who was about a year old at the time. Again, the process took a year, although Alex was from a different orphanage in another part of Bulgaria. This time, somewhere in the process, some lower level official asked their lawyer if "Mr. Brown was a homosexual." The lawyer replied that it was against the law to ask that in the United States and wrong to ask it in Bulgaria; he was a judge, and he should know. "Is this an issue we need to discuss?" Kevin asked the lawyer. "Absolutely not," came the reply; "it's a nonissue."

Alex was a little over two when he arrived home in New York. He was also given the name of a patron saint of Bulgaria and the middle name George. Unlike his older brother, Alex had some separation issues at first. He had bonded closely in his orphanage; in fact, Craig recalls, when Alex was delivered to them, the head of the orphanage had wept. In New York, the same part-time nanny who had helped raise Nikolas was pressed back into service, but "Alex would scream if he couldn't see Craig or me." They sent him to preschool "to keep up the environment he had known in the orphanage," Kevin says, but Kevin had to go along with him, so needy was he at first. Today he's the kid to whom other kids—and grownups—naturally gravitate: slightly theatrical, with honeyed charm, a real salesman.

The brothers are active boys. They swim, go to the beach, love to bike. "There's a constant stream of kids here so they don't need camp," says Craig. "Life is one big play date." They share a large room furnished with a ship with a gangplank; it's a magnet for all the kids. Their apartment overlooks the United Nations garden and the sculpture, a gift of the former Soviet Union, of Saint George slaying a dragon made of missiles. Saint George is another patron saint of Bulgaria, so the view out the window seems again to confirm the Brown-George commitment to preserving their sons' Bulgarian heritage.

Yet this is "the all-American family," says Craig George. "We both have pretty traditional backgrounds, and we share pretty traditional values, and we'll probably do what our families did." Both Kevin's and Craig's parents are doting grandparents, and the boys have lots of cousins. Religion has a strong presence in the household. The boys were baptized Roman Catholic in a rather formal church on Park Avenue, and their fathers agree on the core values of the Church and on a certain structure for bringing up children. "You want to be on as many levels as possible with your kids," says Kevin, "so that we all talk from a shared experience."

Life is busy. The boys are usually either in school or at sports or at speech therapy; their fathers are involved in demanding professions—Craig is a theater director, and Kevin owns and runs a large residential real estate firm. Though Kevin "vowed I would never feed my child McDonald's, now I love to see the place." The family has been to Disneyland, and the fathers look forward to annual ski trips with their sons. At home or away, they wake up with the boys, give them breakfast, have dinner with them, read to them, sing to them, put them to bed, "and hope they have enriched their lives." Their "wonderful nanny" helps, and she provides a female presence for the boys. "Weekends are family time," says Craig—year-round at their weekend home. Kevin and Craig try to go out together once a week—Kevin calls it "Wednesday night date night"—and they also try to "schedule downtime for each of us by ourselves," says Craig.

Neither discrimination nor disapproval seems to be an issue. "It's hard to be in the closet when you have kids," Kevin says. In fact, says Craig, "there are very few gay friends in our circle. Mostly we socialize with other parents. I don't feel like I'm losing anything." The children attend a very nurturing school where their fathers are accepted and embraced, and where there are other gay parents. "We weren't trying to break new ground," Craig says, "just to ensure that our kids would blend in."

But busy as life is, they are careful not to overschedule. While Craig is the sensible, careful parent, Kevin tends to be the goofy one. He likes to take the boys to Grand Central Station, where a long, concrete ramp leads down to the famed Oyster Bar restaurant. He'll put both kids in the stroller, then let it go, running after them as they scream with delight. Then the three of them go down to the train tracks and make believe they're running to catch a train. While everybody stares at them, wondering if they're going to make it or not, the boys yell "All aboard!" and the conductors, clued in to the game, hand the boys their tickets. "We can spend hours down there," says Kevin.

It's the stuff dreams are made on.

The New
American Family

My partner, Barry Miguel, recently announced to me that "only 24 percent of American families are the so-called traditional configuration of mother, father, and kids living under one roof." The implication was that our family—Barry and I, our son and daughter, Zev and Summer, both adopted, both biracial—are part of the majority. "We have two kids, two dogs, and an SUV with three rows of seats to carry us all," Barry says, and he concludes: *"We* are the American family."

Nothing could have been further from our minds when we first got together in early 1993. At the time, we were both happily pursuing interesting careers. Barry, possessing a unique combination of management savvy and inherent creativity, was already well established in the apparel industry, and I, with an interest in not-for-profit public advocacy, was director of fundraising for a gay rights organization. I was 25 and Barry was 38. He had carved out a lifestyle for himself that was both gratifying and fulfilling; I, born in that generation of gay men who felt there were no constraints on us, no limit to our possibilities, thought I had a good sense of the direction I wanted my life to take. It in no way included fatherhood. So many of the men featured in this book talk movingly of having always harbored a yearning for parenthood, of having regretted that coming out, so liberating in so many ways, would—theoretically—close the door on that dream forever. For me at the time, there was no such dream.

Barry and I had a full life that seemed to neither of us to be lacking in any way. We had a nice apartment and a wide circle of friends, availed ourselves of New York's rich cultural opportunities, and even had two dogs, one big, one small.

Granted, we were cushioned by living in a city, New York, whose name is virtually synonymous with diversity and in a neighborhood of that city that has long been a haven for gays. Our life back then was very gay—with a gay doctor, a gay lawyer, and friends who were almost all gay. Still, everyone lives in some version of a community; within the community we inhabited, we flourished.

We were certainly happy together. Over the course of five years as a couple, we weathered two major relocations, an indication that our relationship was mature and stable. The first relocation, to accommodate Barry's work, took us across the country to Portland, Oregon. It was a great career move for Barry, and I was able to find a wonderful job there as well. And Portland, as Barry succinctly puts it, "changed our life."

The people to whom we were drawn in Portland—and the people

who were drawn to us—were folks who shared our tastes and values, reflected our urban sensibilities, had the same interests we had. They were thus in many respects much like the people we had left behind in New York, with one startling difference: almost none of them were gay. In fact, the friends we made in Portland—good friends to this day—were almost all straight couples with young children. There was no method to this, and it was certainly not deliberate; it's just the way things worked out, and it offered us both a fresh context.

After we had been in Portland nearly two years, Barry was transferred again—this time overseas, to Amsterdam. We moved there in early

1997, following our traditional New Year's vacation. It had been our custom, since we met, to spend the holiday with a circle of close friends in some warm place. That year, the place was a villa on a Caribbean island. The setting, overlooking a beautiful beach, was perfect; the villa was equipped with every comfort and convenience; and we were in the company of good friends—10 men in their late thirties and early forties, all in the prime of their careers and at the peak of their powers. Yet in the midst of all this, I felt a sense of personal disquiet, an unsettled, almost displaced feeling.

I was nearing my thirtieth birthday, which I saw as a milestone of sorts, and I had begun to wonder what would happen over the next 30 years, what would bring meaning to my life, and how I would measure my life's value. I thought about my parents, whose lives seemed to me to ring out with rich meaning. At the heart of that richness, as I analyzed it, were their children—my sister and me—and the family that we were. For the first time in my life, I thought about having a child.

So I suggested as much to Barry—whose response was a decided "Absolutely not." He was, he said, in an almost curmudgeonly tone, "too old, too set in my ways, too selfish." He had five nieces whom he loved very much, and he had felt very involved as an uncle, but fatherhood, he insisted, "is *not* what I want to do." I retreated. "All right," I told Barry. "I won't fight you on this." I put fatherhood on the back burner of my life, where it hovered. As for Barry, the idea of children had been planted in his mind, and to the surprise of us both, it began to ripen.

On a business trip in the spring of 1997, Barry took time for dinner with longtime friends, a gay couple who had recently adopted a son from Romania. Both the boy and his parents were flourishing. Their happiness made a strong case for the idea of adoption, and when Barry returned to Amsterdam, he brought the names and phone numbers of a few Stateside adoption agencies.

I took on the task of preliminary research, dialed the first agency on the list, and told them I was calling for a consult, explaining that I was part of a same-sex couple. Within three minutes, the executive director said to me: "We have a birthmother I think you would like. I think she would like you, too. She is due in two months, and the baby will most likely be biracial. Here's her number. Give her a call. You have twenty-four hours to decide."

We were giddy with excitement at the possibility of becoming parents. We called her, we liked her, and she liked us, so we hired a lawyer and made the match. And suddenly, now that it was happening, we wondered if it could really be this easy, if it was really possible that we were going to become fathers in 60 days.

But the process from then on was by no means hassle free. We suffered through some of the same frustrations and fears as so many of the other men in this book, shared the same worries and concerns. Would the baby be healthy? Would the birthmother go through with the placement? Were we up to the task of parenthood? The birthmother said she was seven months pregnant, but a prenatal checkup showed she was only two months pregnant. Was this an innocent miscalculation or bad faith? None of the doctors treating the birthmother would return repeated calls from me and Barry, even though the birthmother had granted us medical consent. Were they busy or hostile or was it something else altogether? And when a phone call alerted us to a potential medical disaster, we sweated through those middle-of-the-night terrors till we heard the birthmother

and baby were fine. I learned an important lesson from all this—that sometimes, it's not the journey that counts, it's the destination.

As the pregnancy progressed, we learned that we would have a son; February 13, 1998, was pinpointed as the due date. We decided our son needed a name that would be different—since he would be biracial; strong—since he would have two gay dads; and reflective of his Jewish upbringing. We decided on Zev, Hebrew for "wolf."

That holiday season, Barry and I took our usual warm-weather vacation—just the two of us this time—in Bali. I had made a collage out of magazine photos of scores of biracial babies—the thing was about two feet by a foot and a half—and had tacked onto it lots of positive affirmations.

Healthy Baby! it read. Love! Welcome! I made a sort of shrine of the collage, and every day, I burned incense in front of it, lit candles, and prayed. I also paid a Hindu priestess to perform a ceremony said to ensure a safe birth. We had already gone through a dozen books on child-rearing and had signed up for classes on baby massage, diaper-changing, and the care and feeding of infants. I was covering all the bases, leaving no stone unturned in my search for a guarantee—impossible, of course—of a healthy baby that his birthmother would willingly place with us. After living through seven months of a pregnancy, I was totally emotionally invested in this baby. It seemed I had spent every waking moment thinking about being his father; still unborn, he held me by an extraordinary bond.

We flew back from Bali to Amsterdam—an 18-hour flight—and were sound asleep when the phone rang. It was our birthmother's sister calling: The birthmother was in labor five and a half weeks early, and we should come quickly. The news frightened us. We caught the next flight to New York, then another flight upstate. The baby had not yet been born. It was as if the birthmother had waited for us. And the baby had, too.

Our son was born the next day. Barry and I were outside the delivery room, but we could hear the birthmother scream and groan. "I can't push anymore!" she insisted. "Just one more," the doctor urged. More groaning. Then silence. A few moments later, the nurses wheeled out a tiny and beautiful baby: Zev.

Our joy was overwhelming. After seven months of planning and worrying, we were parents. Or close, anyway. We were still concerned about Zev's health, and we had a run-in with the hospital social worker who was not happy to have two men laying claim to this child. And since, in New York State, until a child leaves the hospital, its mother continues to retain parental rights, we worried that something could still go wrong legally.

Zev remained in the hospital for two weeks until his sucking mechanism matured—which is normal in premature births—and we were there the whole time. The hospital staff in this small town were leery at first of these two gay men who thought themselves fathers, but as we—and members of our family—stood by each day, holding Zev, feeding him, bathing him, changing him, reading to him, they grew convinced that Zev belonged to us and we to him. We took him home to New York for a *brit,* the Jewish circumcision ceremony, attended by all five grandparents and lots of friends, and then flew with him back to Amsterdam.

I took parental leave for three months. As a preemie, Zev needed frequent feedings. I was seriously sleep-deprived till he was nine months old. Yet the bond I had felt for him before his birth was as real as I imagined it—even more so. Some of the happiest times of my life were just being with him, maybe sitting in a café—me with a cup of coffee, Zev with his bottle—or taking a walk snuggling him in the front-pack, or just being at home holding him. It was a wonderful love I would not have missed for anything.

Of course, Barry felt the same. And among other joys, fatherhood added an entirely new dimension to our relationship. It unleashed the parenting instinct in both of us that Barry insists is "as real as the maternal instinct, but less realized." And of course, it took us out of ourselves. I used to think the world consisted of gay and nongay; now I see it as people without kids and people with kids. From here, our old, self-absorbed lifestyle seems light-years away.

Zev was about nine months old when we came back to the United States. A year or so later, we began to think about having a second child.

We felt it important that Zev should have someone with whom he could share his very particular experience; as we saw it, being biracial, Jewish, and the child of two gay men represented a lot of pressure on an only child. I also felt an almost spiritual imperative, a cosmic insistence that there was another child out there who was fated to be part of our family. Barry again had reservations about bringing another child into our lives— but again he came around.

And again, the process was pitted with challenges. In fact, it was tougher this time. There was the sleeping infant boy we held for two hours, who never woke up and who simply didn't feel like our child; he was soon adopted by another gay couple that had bonded with him in-

stantly. There was the birthmother due in a few weeks to whom we wired money for living expenses; we never heard from her or our money again. There was the homeless birthmother I took to her first prenatal care in seven months of pregnancy with her two toddlers in tow. A week later, on Mother's Day, she gave birth prematurely and changed her mind about placing her baby with us.

Finally, however, in June 2001, on a lovely day that hinted of a beautiful summer to come, we got the call that our daughter had been born. We named her Summer.

Of course, we feared, as every parent does, that our second child couldn't possibly be as perfect as our first, and that we couldn't possibly love her as much. And of course, both fears evaporated in a split second. Summer is totally different from Zev, and it has been wonderful to discover her—a really tough little girl with big brown ringlets touched with blond, assertive, very smart, physically active, and her own person. One day when Zev thought he'd really rather not have Summer share the book he and I were reading, she climbed up and simply sat down on the book. It certainly worked, and it was quintessentially *her*—and very un-Zev. In fact, about the only thing that is the same about Zev and Summer is the love Barry and I feel for them.

For the most part, Zev reacted well to having a sister. He was three and a half years older, after all, and had a busy life: friends, preschool, camp. He wanted to know if the baby had come from my tummy but was satisfied to hear she had come from a birth mommy, just as he had. Zev knows that his birth mommy was unable to care for him and instead had set out to find two men who would be his "forever daddies," as we tell his story. His birthmother's photo is framed on the wall with other family photographs, but he doesn't ask about her often.

Our life changed in another way when Summer was born. When we had first moved back to New York after living in what Barry calls the "mixed worlds" of Portland and Amsterdam, we had gravitated back to our old Greenwich Village crowd. In the gay community, says Barry, "we were a novelty. We had been away, we had a child, and he was very cute. We got invitations from people we hadn't seen in years. Within our circle, after all, we were pioneers. There weren't that many gay men who had adopted a child." But once our daughter Summer arrived, he goes on, "that was it—the final wedge between us and the gay community."

The reason? "We were a family," Barry says, "your basic American family, and we were now not so interesting. When one kid is running around and a baby is screaming, the novelty has worn off—at least where others are concerned."

Neither of us misses the life that has left us. One Halloween, when we were marching with Zev in a kids' parade, we ran into two old friends of Barry's and stopped to chat. Says Barry: "They had all the right fashion accessories—the latest Prada jacket, the latest Nikes, the latest Gucci belts—they were on their way to an antique show, and I thought: 'I have just passed my former life, and I am so much happier in the life I've chosen.'"

Barry continues to work full time, and I am a full-time parent. We try to go "on a date" Saturday nights, but otherwise, we're pretty hands-on parents who are equally nurturing; the usual gender role separations don't apply. Our children, as Barry says, are the "beneficiaries of all the hard work done by people over the years"—the struggles and victories of gay rights activists and other fighters for tolerance—and we think they are fortunate to grow up in an environment of varying family configurations. When our preschooler son was taunted by a classmate for being adopted and having two dads, Zev kept his cool and refused to be baited. "I'm adopted too," the classmate finally said, although he is not, then turned his attention elsewhere. Obviously, no parent can be there every time a child is teased or picked on, nor should we be. My goal as a parent is to empower our children and give them self-esteem—the tools with which they can get through anything. That's the best way I know of to protect and nurture them.

I'll always remember what the judge said to Barry and me the day we finalized Zev's adoption. "I can see there's a lot of love between the two of you this day," he told us, his white hair and black robe lending even more authority to his words. "But I want you to know that if things ever change, you are each legally responsible for this child for the rest of your lives." It struck me then—it strikes me now—that this is the most powerful, most unbreakable bond two gay men can have. We can register as domestic partners, have civil union ceremonies, break up, buy and sell joint property, tussle over joint possessions. But this bond—being fathers to our children—is unbreakable, and it is forever.

FATHERS AND THEIR FAMILIES:

WHO'S WHO IN THE PHOTOGRAPHS

(from left to right)

Adoption The complete legal transfer of parental rights and obligations from one family—usually the birth family—to the adoptive family, which then assumes all the legal obligations and responsibilities for the child.

Adoption agencies Organizations licensed by a state to place children with adoptive families.

Adoption attorneys Lawyers who specialize in adoption. Their actions range from handling legal paperwork to assisting adoptive parents with all or most of the adoption process.

Adoption facilitators Often social workers, often unlicensed experts, adoption facilitators identify birthmothers, write adoption résumés, deal with birthmother meetings, and in other ways help people to adopt a child. Some states outlaw the practice.

Agency adoption An adoption arranged by social workers at a licensed adoption agency, whether public or private.

Birthmother, birthfather, birthparents The biological parents of an adopted child.

Coparenting Shared parenting. Although the phrase evolved to cover joint custody parenting by divorced former spouses, for gay biological fathers it typically means sharing custody and/or parenting with the child's birthmother, usually after a birth by traditional surrogacy.

Domestic adoption Adopting a child from his/her country of origin. In the United States it is the adoption of a child by an American.

Egg donor The woman who sells or gives her eggs to be used to create an embryo.

Finalization The court proceeding giving full legal status to the adopter as a child's parent; a new updated birth certificate is typically issued.

Foster-adopt, Fost-adopt, Fos-adopt Short for foster-adoptive, in which the prospective adoptive child moves into the applicant's home on a foster care basis before he or she is legally freed. A fost-adopt placement typically offers a higher likelihood of being matched with a child.

Foster child   A child in the custody of a governmental or private adoption agency who can be adopted when a judge terminates the parental rights of the biological parents or they voluntarily relinquish those rights.

Foster parent   The person who cares for a child legally in the custody of the state or county. Typically, foster parents must be screened, trained, and evaluated before being licensed by the state or county to care for children temporarily in their home. Foster parents care for a child until he or she can be returned to the birth family, or until he or she is freed for adoption, at which time the foster family is often the first choice for adoptive placement.

Homestudy, Family study   The evaluation process that approves or disapproves prospective parents for adoption. The process typically includes interviews and documentation on such issues as health, finances, employment, and medical status. Prospective parents may be interviewed about their family life, challenges, and struggles, and how they cope with difficult experiences. In addition, a physical "walk-through" of the prospective parents' home ensures that it meets such basic safety standards as working smoke alarms and security features. A homestudy may take four to six months to complete.

Implantation   Embedding a fertilized egg into the endometrium (mucous membrane lining) of the uterus.

In vitro fertilization   An assisted reproductive procedure in which an egg is removed from a ripe follicle and fertilized by a sperm cell outside of the human body. The fertilized egg divides in a protected environment for about two days and then is inserted into the uterus of the woman who produced the egg or into a surrogate.

Independent adoption   A nonagency or private adoption.

International adoption   Adopting a child from another country. Many countries do not allow openly gay men to adopt.

Legal guardian   The person legally responsible for a child. This might be one or both adoptive parents before adoption is finalized.

MAPP (Model Approach to Partnerships in Parenting)   Training, often required, that prepares prospective adoptive or foster parents to bring a child or children into their lives.

Open adoption   An adoption in which the adopting parents and the birthparents agree on whether and how to continue contact between them.

Photo listing   Picture albums, often also available on-line, of children legally freed for adoption in a specific state. A national photo listing of children available for adoption, www.adoptuskids.org, is an initiative of the Children's Bureau of the Administration for Children and Families, U.S. Department of Health and Human Services, and is operated by the National Adoption Center.

Public adoption agencies   State social services agencies run by state or county governments that typically deal with foster children, a significant percentage of whom may be available for adoption.

Readoption   After adopting their child in the country of his or her birth, parents adopting internationally readopt the child a second time before a U.S. judge.

Second-parent adoption   While legally married couples can adopt a child together, couples not legally married typically cannot. In the latter case, therefore, the child will be adopted first by one parent and then by the second parent.

Semiopen adoption   An adoption in which the parties exchange only nonidentifying information.

Social worker, Caseworker   The worker bees of adoption, social workers typically conduct a homestudy and follow-up visits once a child is placed. They may also interview prospective parents, identify potential adoptees, and provide support and education.

Special-needs children   Children with illnesses or handicaps or who face problems or circumstances that make them "hard to place."

Surrogacy (gestational)   A process in which a woman carries and delivers a baby to whom she is not genetically related. The embryos implanted in a gestational surrogate are typically formed of the eggs of an egg donor fertilized in vitro by the sperm of one or both gay fathers.

Surrogacy (traditional)   A process in which a woman, using her own eggs, is artificially inseminated with the semen of the prospective father. She then carries and gives birth to the child.

Surrogate   A woman who serves as a "host uterus," gestating an embryo that is not genetically related to her, then relinquishing the child to its genetic and/or adoptive parent(s).

RESOURCES

WHERE TO START

HRC FamilyNet

Human Rights Campaign (HRC) FamilyNet is the most comprehensive and up-to-date resource on gay, lesbian, bisexual, and transgender (GLBT) families. HRC FamilyNet provides extensive information
and resources about adoption, foster care, and surrogacy, including a step-
by-step process to adopt domestically or internationally, an overview of
states that currently appear to be open to or tolerant of gay adoptions, and
a state-by-state listing of gay-friendly adoption agencies and attorneys.
Make HRC FamilyNet your first stop. And when you become a parent,

HRC FamilyNet also offers a wealth of information and resources to address issues particular to GLBT parents.

website: www.HRC.org/familynet

ADOPTION: INFORMATION, HELP, REFERRALS

North American Council on Adoptable Children
Founded in 1974 by adoptive parents, the North American Council on Adoptable Children is committed to meeting the needs of waiting children and the families who adopt them.

970 Raymond Avenue, Suite 106
St. Paul, MN 55114
phone: (651) 644-3036
fax: (651) 644-9848
email: info@nacac.org
website: www.nacac.org

National Adoption Information Clearinghouse
A comprehensive resource on all aspects of adoption.

330 C Street SW
Washington, DC 20447
phone: (888) 251-0075 or (703) 352-3488
fax: (703) 385-3206
email: NAIC@calib.com
web: www.calib.com/naic

Child Welfare League of America

The oldest and largest national nonprofit that develops and promotes policies and programs to protect American children and strengthen America's families.

440 First Street NW, Third Floor
Washington, DC 20001-2085
phone: (202) 638-2952

National Adoption Center

A nonprofit organization whose mission is to expand adoption opportunities throughout the United States for children with special needs and those from minority cultures.

1500 Walnut Street, No. 701
Philadelphia, PA 19102
phone: (800) TO-ADOPT
website: www.nationaladoptioncenter.org or www.adopt.org

National Council for Adoption

Organization with goal of helping as many children as possible find permanent homes through adoption.

1930 17th Street NW
Washington, DC 20009
phone: (202) 328-1200
website: www.ucfa-usa.org

Adopt Us Kids

Dedicated to finding permanent, loving, adoptive families for the thousands of U.S. children who are currently waiting in foster care. Adopt Us Kids is a national database with photos of children awaiting adoption and families approved to adopt. The AdoptUsKids website allows families to search for children and workers to search for families throughout the United States. You can "meet the children" by going on the website.

Adoption Exchange Association
8015 Corporate Drive, Suite C
Baltimore, MD 21236
phone: (800) 901-6911
website: www.adoptuskids.org

Pact

A nonprofit organization whose primary mission is "to serve children of color in need of adoption or who are growing up in adoptive families," Pact has set out to create the most comprehensive website addressing issues for adopted children of color, including many useful resources on transracial adoption. Pact has helped place more than 450 children in permanent, loving families and has counseled thousands of adopted adults, birthparents, foster parents, and adoptive parents.

Beth Hall, codirector
Pact, An Adoption Alliance
3220 Blume Drive, Suite 289
Richmond, CA 94806
phone: (510) 243-9460

fax: (510) 243-9970

books and education: (866) 722-8257

birthparent line: (800) 750-7590

adoptive parent peer support: (888) 448-8277

email: info@pactadopt.org

website: www.pactadopt.org

INTERNATIONAL ADOPTION

U.S. State Department/Consular Affairs

The online brochure "International Adoptions" provides both information and guidance to U.S. citizens seeking information about international adoptions.

Or contact:

Department of State

Office of Children's Issues (CA/OCS/CI)

2201 C Street NW

SA-22, Room 2100

Washington, DC 20520-4818

phone: (202) 736-7000

fax: (202) 312-9743

autofax: (202) 647-3000

internet address: http://travel.state.gov

toll-free number: (888) 407-4747

National Foster Parent Association

An organization started by and composed of foster parents whose mission is to strengthen foster families through publications, training, and education; to carry out nationally focused legislative advocacy; and to provide opportunities for networking.

7512 Stanich Avenue, No. 6
Gig Harbor, WA 98335
phone: (800) 557-5238
website: www.nfpainc.org

Casey Family Programs

Recruits and licenses foster parents in 14 states, mostly west of the Mississippi.

1300 Dexter Avenue N., Third Floor
Seattle, WA 98109-3542
phone: (800) 228-3559, (206) 282-7300, 282-3330
fax: (206) 282-3555
website: www.casey.org

National Resource Center for Foster Care and Permanency Planning

Training, technical assistance, and information services to help child welfare agencies. Affiliated with Hunter College School of Social Work.

129 E. 79th Street
New York, NY 10021
phone: (212) 452-7043
fax: (212) 452-7051

SURROGACY

Growing Generations
The pioneer gay-focused surrogacy agency.

5757 Wilshire Boulevard, Suite 601
Los Angeles, CA 90036
phone: (323) 965-7500
fax: (323) 965-0900
email: family@GrowingGenerations.com
website: www.GrowingGenerations.com

GAY PARENTING ORGANIZATIONS

Center Kids
Center Kids is a program run by New York City's Lesbian, Gay, Bisexual, and Transgender Community Center to advocate at state and local levels for the rights of alternative families.

The Lesbian and Gay Community Services Center, Inc.
208 W. 13th Street
New York, NY 10011
phone: (212) 620-7310
website: www.gaycenter.org

COLAGE
COLAGE (Children of Lesbian and Gays Everywhere) fosters "the growth of daughters and sons of lesbian, gay, bisexual and transgender

parents of all racial, ethnic, and class backgrounds by providing education, support and community on local and international levels, to advocate for our rights and those of our families, and to promote acceptance and awareness that love makes a family." State-by-state gay fathers groups; sponsors annual Family Weeks, one in Provincetown, Massachusetts, the other in Saugatuck, Michigan.

3543 18th Street, No. 1
San Francisco, CA 94110
phone: (415) 861-KIDS (5437)
fax: (415) 255-8345
email: colage@colage.org
website: www.colage.org

Family Pride Coalition

Advancing the well-being of lesbian, gay, bisexual, and transgendered parents and their families. The best way to connect with other GLBT families.

PO Box 65327
Washington, DC 20035-5327
phone: (202) 331-5015
fax: (202) 331-0080
website: www.familypride.org

Gay and Lesbian Adoptive Family Project

A study by the Florida State University School of Social Work to learn more about GLBT individuals and couples who have adopted at least one child.

phone: (888) 290-3155

email: gladoptions@hotmail.com

Rainbow Families

A membership organization working to organize and strengthen GLBT parents and children in the upper Midwest, serving more than 1,500 families. Rainbow Families provides parents and prospective parents with resources, education, and support so they can build strong families and openly confront society's injustices. RF provides public education and advocacy in the larger communities to transform the institutions that affect our lives.

711 W. Lake Street, Suite 210
Minneapolis, MN 55408
phone: (612) 827-7731
website: www.rainbowfamilies.org

ADOPTION AGENCIES USED BY THE
FAMILIES IN THIS BOOK

Family Builders

528 Grand Avenue
Oakland, CA 94610
phone: (510) 272-0204
fax: (510) 272-0277
email: kids@familybuilders.com

Family Focus

54-40 Little Neck Parkway
Little Neck, NY 11362
phone: (718) 224-1919
website: www.familyfocusadoption.org

Friends in Adoption

44 South Street
PO Box 1228
Middletown Springs, VT 05757-1228
phone: (802) 235-2373, (800) 844-3630
email: fia@friendsinadoption.org

Friends in Adoption International

The Maltex Building
431 Pine Street, No. 7
Burlington, VT 05401
phone: (802) 865-9886

Black Adoption Services

Three Rivers Adoption Council
307 Fourth Avenue, Suite 710
Pittsburgh, PA 15222
phone: (412) 471-8722
fax: (412) 471-4861
website: www.3riversadopt.org

ADOPTION ATTORNEYS/SPECIALISTS

Suzanne Nichols, Esq.

70 W. Red Oak Lane
White Plains, NY 10604
phone: (914) 697-4870
fax: (914) 697-4888
email: adoptnpro@aol.com

Michael Goldstein, Esq.

62 Bowman Avenue
Rye Brook, NY 10573
phone: (914) 939-1111

Nancy Hurwitz Kors, Ph.D.

1844 San Miguel Drive, Suite 310
Walnut Creek, CA 94596
phone: (925) 938-6600
website: www.adopt-now.com

OTHER

AFFIRM: Psychologists Affirming their Gay, Lesbian, and Bisexual Family
A network of psychologists with gay, lesbian, or bisexual relatives. Provides open support for their own family members, supports clinical

and research work within psychology, and encourages sensitivity to the role of sexual orientation in all clinical and research work.

SUNY Psychology Dept.
Stony Brook, NY 11794-2500

And Baby Magazine
And Baby Magazine envisions a community of readers with unique parenting options to consider and social issues to address. Six issues per year.

Los Angeles, Calif.
phone: (323) 957-0979
website: www.andbabymag.com

In the Family Magazine
In the Family is an award-winning quarterly magazine that explores the complex interweave of gay, lesbian, bisexual, transgender, and straight family bonds. Engaging and intelligent, it examines the richness and challenges of negotiating diversity within families. Most contributors are mental health professionals of all sexual orientations who have expertise helping our families.

In the Family Magazine
7850 N. Silverbell Road, Suite 114–188
Tucson, AZ 85743
phone: (520) 579-8043
website: www.inthefamily.com
subscription information: $24/year for our quarterly magazine

Let Him Stay

Produced by the ACLU Lesbian & Gay Rights Project to fight Florida's gay and lesbian adoption ban, this is an interactive up-to-date website detailing the story of the Lofton Family in Florida whose son the state is trying to remove from the family setting.

website: www.lethimstay.com

Daddy & Papa

Video produced and directed by Johnny Symons showing heart-warming examples of the Gay Dads phenomenon.

Persistent Visions
PO Box 3486
Berkeley, CA 94703
phone: (510) 653-8763
fax: (510) 653-8783
email: Symon@ix.netcom.com
website: www.daddyandpapa.com

THE COST OF CREATING A FAMILY:

ESTIMATES IN 2002 DOLLARS

What did you pay for your car? How did you finance it? When you think about creating your family, think in those terms.

Maris Blechner, executive director,
Family Focus adoption agency

For public adoption and foster care, there should be no cost. For special-needs adoption or fostering, in fact, subsidies are typically available. Contact the North American Council on Adoptable Children (see Resources) at www.nacac.org.

The cost for an independent or private domestic adoption will differ from state to state. Again, check with NACAC for your state. Typically, however, given the involvement of one or more lawyers, count on a range of from $5,000 to $20,000.

For an international adoption, the costs may range from $15,000 to $20,000, but again, the costs differ from country to country and situation to situation.

The costs for traditional surrogacy range from $40,000 to $65,000; for gestational surrogacy the costs can run from $75,000 to $100,000.

DAVID STRAH left full-time work as a professional fundraiser for various nonprofit organizations to become a full-time father when his son was born in 1998. The constant questions he was asked—"How did you do it? What is it like?"—as well as his feeling that there were stories like his that needed to be told inspired him to write *Gay Dads: A Celebration of Fatherhood.* He lives with Barry Miguel, his partner of more than a decade, together with their son, Zev, and daughter, Summer, in New York City.

Contact: david@gaydads.info

KRIS TIMKEN has been a working photographer since the early 1980s. She has a BA from Stanford University and a BFA with distinction in photography from California College of Arts and Crafts.

Contact: kris@ktimken.net

SUSANNA MARGOLIS is the author of the adventure travel guides *Walking Europe From Top to Bottom* and *Adventuring in the Pacific,* and she is a contributor to *The Sierra Club Guides to the National Parks: California, Hawaii, and American Samoa.* She is coauthor, with Judith Dunford, of the novel *Cashing In* under the joint pen name Antonia Gowar. She has also cowritten nearly a dozen works of nonfiction. She lives in New York City.